What Four

Family Fruitcake Frenzy
Book Four in the Val Fremden Mystery Series
Margaret Lashley

Copyright 2017 Margaret Lashley

Praise for the Val Fremden Series

"My cheeks hurt from laughing at the outrageously hilarious situations that Val gets into. Holidays with crazy family members, and the redneck mentality were a hoot and so very accurate. This series is my absolute favorite."

"In a style much like Janet Evanovich, her characters leave you laughing out loud and find you wishing to meet them."

"I haven't laughed this hard in a while. Val's mother and aunts are hoots. People, you've got to read this book!"

"It doesn't get much better than this. Another crazy romp through Val land."

"I laughed, and cried, until tears ran down my cheeks with both. My heart swelled with joy, my gut clenched with pain. I wanted to reach into the book and hug Val like she was a long lost sister."

"To find a book that is both hilarious and tear jerking is somewhat of a rarity and to find an author that produces such books is just as rare. From laughing one minute to being emotional the next, this book is fantastic!!! I recommend this book and the entire series."

More Hilarious Val Fremden Mysteries

by Margaret Lashley
Absolute Zero
Glad One
Two Crazy
Three Dumb
What Four
Five Oh
Six Tricks
Seven Daze
Figure Eight
Cloud Nine

"If you want to know how far you've evolved as a person, go visit your mother."
Val Fremden

Chapter One

FOR FOLKS WHO CALLED the lower half of Florida home, the winter holidays always arrived without warning. We didn't have harbingers like frosty mornings or falling leaves. Instead, like a maladjusted mugger, one day when we least expected it Old Saint Nick ran up beside us, kicked us in the gut, and left us reeling with dread.

Or maybe it was just me....

THE LAST DAY OF NOVEMBER was one of those perfect days that made St. Petersburg the envy of every tourist north of the Florida state line. The sky was a cloudless, robin's-egg blue, the temperature was under 80 degrees, and the humidity was actually bearable for a change. There was only one fly in this perfect ointment. It was a four-letter word called "work."

Well, screw that.

Instead of heading to the office, I unhooked my bra, tugged on a bathing suit, turned off my cellphone, and headed for Sunset Beach.

I squandered my stolen morning wading the shoreline, the breeze in my hair and the sugar-white sand between my toes. Small whitecaps dotted the normally lolling surf. As a native to the Sunshine State, I knew the stronger waves meant better shelling. I peered into the clear Gulf water and reached toward a shape in the roiling break line. I pulled up a beautiful, left-handed whelk shell and smiled. It was a rare oddity, kind of like my beach combing days of late.

Even though summer had eased into a more bearable not-quite-summer mode, the sun never relented this far south in Florida. I pressed an index finger to my shoulder and released it. A circle of white appeared on my skin, then evaporated into bright pink. I was half-cooked. I decided to pack it in for the day before I resembled the boiled-lobster tourists sprawled out in their beach chairs.

As I slipped through the picket fence surrounding the parking lot of Caddy's beach bar, a sudden flash of naughtiness added swagger to my steps. It cost five dollars to park at Caddy's. But last year, when I'd been flat broke, I'd discovered that the lot attendant didn't arrive to collect money until 8 a.m. Ever since, I'd made a point of getting there early enough to beat the fee. I grinned like a petty thief. The five bucks I'd saved could buy a lot of tonic for my Tanqueray.

The top was down on Maggie, my 1963 Ford Falcon Sprint. I tested the red leatherette upholstery with a wet fingertip. It almost sizzled. *Yow!* I lay a beach towel over the bucket seat and tugged a yellow gingham sundress over my one-piece bathing suit. I settled into the seat, set my hands on the steering wheel, straightened my shoulders, and took a deep breath of salty beach air.

Ahh! What could possibly make this day any better?

Only one thing came to mind. I smiled and turned the ignition key. Then, just for fun, I mashed the gas pedal down. Maggie's twin glass-pack muffler rumbled like a baritone with bronchitis. As I exited the lot, Maggie instinctively turned left toward Gulf Boulevard, the main beach drag. It cut through the middle of a thin split of land rimmed with gorgeous, white-sand beaches that were the envy of the world.

After driving past a long string of pastel-colored, low-slung mom-and-pop hotels and junky souvenir shops, I steered Maggie right, onto Central Avenue. I hit the gas again, and in a few minutes we were in downtown St. Petersburg, the location of my favorite guilty pleasure – Chocolateers.

Chocolate pusher-man Jack was there to greet me when I walked into the shop.

He grinned at me and shook his head. "The usual, Val?"

I nodded, and slid a wilted five-dollar bill across the glass-topped display counter. Jack eyed the money, then reached into the case and retrieved two dark-brown confections the size of walnuts. He put the beautiful, hand-made chocolates onto a paper napkin and gingerly placed them on the counter. Jack's eyes said a longing goodbye to his handiwork, then he took a step back and cringed.

I grabbed the hand-dipped, chocolate-covered cherries and crammed them both into my mouth like a starving hobo. As I bit down, their hard shells popped inside my mouth like sweet, red grapes.

Mmmm.

This chocolate addict had just gotten her fix.

AS I LEFT CHOCOLATEERS, I turned my cellphone back on. The clock registered 11 a.m. That meant I still had some time to kill before lunch. I decided to cruise along the downtown waterfront district. I was idling at the corner of 4th Avenue and Beach Drive when the inevitable happened.

Old St. Nick got me.

On an open stretch of grass in Straub Park, about a dozen guys in shorts and t-shirts were toiling together like ants. I stared, slack-jawed, as they pulled to standing the City of St Petersburg's humongous artificial Christmas tree.

It may as well have been a forty-foot-tall effigy of my mother's scowling face.

A chill ran down my spine despite the heat. Panic shot through me. Soon, I'd be obliged to keep a promise I'd made months ago in a moment of sniveling weakness. I'd be forced to visit my mother for the holidays.

A horn honked behind me, startling me out of my stupor. I made a hasty left onto Beach Drive. An old, familiar knot gripped my stomach. Its name was Lucille Jolly. Lucille was my adoptive mother – a fact I'd discovered less than two years ago. Up until then, I thought she'd been the real thing. As shocked as I'd been to find out Lucille wasn't my biological mother, the news had, in the end, left me feeling *relieved.*

It meant I hadn't come from her gene pool.

I supposed everyone had a love-hate relationship with their mother. Since I'd only known Glad Goldrich, my true mother, for six weeks before she'd died, we'd never gotten around to the hate part. But on *that* score, Lucille and I'd had almost fifty years of dutiful practice.

And in a few weeks, I would get even more.

My brain turned to mush. My arms went leaden. I took a slow and aimless drive along North Shore Boulevard as if I'd run out of gas. To my left, sunlight danced like a billion bright diamonds on the wide expanse of Tampa Bay. To my right, the huge oaks of Vinoy Park spread their arms above manicured flowerbeds. But I couldn't see the beauty. My eyes were clouded by impending doom. I pulled into a parking spot and blew out a huge breath.

The mere thought of having to spend time with Lucille Jolly drained me like a used-up battery. The woman knew all my buttons and how to push them. Hell, she should've. She'd pretty much installed every one of them. Like a snowball in Florida, I didn't have a chance in hell against her mysterious ability to instantly vaporize my self-esteem.

My mood shot, I was about to head home when my cellphone rang. It was my cop boyfriend, Tom.

"Hey you," he said. "What 'cha doing?"

"Thinking of running away and joining the circus."

Tom laughed. "Sorry, Val. You're not weird enough."

"Tell that to Lucille."

"Uh-oh. Already getting worked up about the trip?"

"How'd you guess?"

"Val, it's only for a few days. Family is family. You're stuck with them, whether you like it or not."

I pursed my lips. Even though Tom had already met my mother, it'd been a brief encounter. He'd yet to make the acquaintance of any of my other relatives. This had not been unintentional on my part. My family was a croaker-sack full of crazy. At the best of times, they were comic relief. At the worst of times...well, that was the stuff of legends.

And then there were...*the holidays.*

The mere thought of the word caused my heart to palpitate.

Christmas was to the Jolly clan what a full moon was to a pack of rabid werewolves. Tom had no idea the level of lunacy he was getting himself into.

"Family is family all right," I said. "Don't remind me."

"Hey. I'm going with you. It'll be fun."

I blew out a tired sigh.

"Yeah, sure Tom. It's gonna be a blast."

Chapter Two

NEARLY TEN YEARS AGO, I'd had a thriving copy-writing business. Then I'd turned forty and totally freaked out. Convinced I'd become nothing more than an invisible cog in a pointless machine, I'd ditched my entire life and run off to Europe. In Germany, I did a seven-year stint as an ex-pat, a foreigner's wife, and a would-be house renovator. When that fell apart two years ago, I'd returned to St. Pete as a broke ex-wife in dire need of renovation myself.

As I crammed my toes into my work heels to face another Friday morning at the office, a thought stopped me in my tracks. *Everything had come full circle.* Here I was again, just a cog in the pointless accounting firm of Griffith & Maas.

No, no, no!

I shook my head to clear the cobwebs clogging my brain.

I can't let myself turn into that sad, angry, robot woman again! If I do...holy crap! That would mean I'd wasted my entire forties! Lord knows I don't have another decade to squander!

A scowl dug itself into my face as I stuffed my feet into my pumps. I stomped to the bathroom and made a final check of my face and hair in the mirror. One glance and I felt as deflated as a leaky balloon.

When did I start looking like Lucille? Geeze! She's not even my mother! This isn't fair at all!

I marched into the kitchen, flung open the cupboard, and took a slug of spiced rum straight from the bottle. Fortified for the day, I scrounged my car keys from between the sofa cushions, grabbed my purse, and headed out the door.

WHEN I ARRIVED AT GRIFFITH & Maas, Milly wasn't too happy to see me. For the past six months, my best friend had also become my boss. I'd filled the receptionist position left open when the skunk-haired, crack-addicted Mrs. Barnes had retired under "extenuating circumstances."

I supposed as my manager it was Milly's job to remain somewhat at arm's length and disgruntled with me. I understood that. But I didn't have to like it. Even though Milly had gotten me the job in the first place, the idea that she was my superior still rubbed me in all the wrong places – like sand in the bottom of my bathing suit.

"Missed you yesterday," Milly said as I walked in the door. Her voice was more accusatory than concerned. "Were you sick?"

"In a way, yeah." I dropped my purse on my desk and copped an attitude. "Look, Milly. I was all caught up with the filing and scheduling. And you didn't have any appointments yesterday. So I took a mental health day."

Milly scowled. "Val, would it have killed you to check with me first?"

I scrunched my eyebrows together and shrugged. "Yeah, maybe."

Milly sighed, weary of my crap. "Listen. I know getting back in the workforce has been an adjustment for you, Val. But I need you to follow some rules. Color inside the lines once in a while. I thought I had you trained better."

A red-hot shot of rebellion raced through me. "*Trained me?*"

"You know what I mean. Val, this 'free-spirit' bull crap is starting to wear thin."

I knew Milly was right. And it made me even madder. I should have been grateful. She'd put herself out on a limb with Mr. Maas when she'd recommended me as her personal assistant. To be fair, I *did* have fleeting moments of gratitude. But for the most part, I just felt trapped. Even so, I had no one to blame for my ensnarement but myself. It wasn't as if Milly had kidnapped me, stolen my money and chained me to a desk, after all. I'd managed to screw up my life without her assistance.

"Sorry, Milly. You're right," I said with a tad less sarcasm. "I promise to schedule all my future crises beforehand."

Milly shot me a hurt, angry glance. She turned to leave. I felt like a crap.

"Milly?"

She turned around, exasperated. "What?"

"I didn't mean that like it sounded. I'm serious. I'll try to be more responsible."

Milly smiled, but her eyes didn't brighten. "Thanks."

"You going out with Vance tonight?" I asked.

The mention of her new boyfriend made Milly's face light up.

She looked me up and down, uncertainty twisting her tentative smile. "Yes. Now, get to work, will you?"

I saluted. "Yes ma'am. You can count on me."

Chapter Three

TWO WEEKS HAD PASSED since St. Pete's forty-foot Christmas tree had sapped away most of my will to live. On the bright side, I'd finally found something to appreciate about my menial job. It offered temporary distraction from my obsessive thoughts about something even worse – the impending holiday hoedown in Hicksville, also known as Christmas at my mother's place.

"Do you like fruitcake?" I asked Tom.

He was leaning against the frame of my front door, looking just as I always pictured him in my daydreams. His crisp, white shirt was rolled up to his elbows. It seemed to glow in contrast to his golden-tan skin. Tom's fresh-pressed blue jeans were snug in all the right places, held up with a simple leather belt. And his sea-green eyes were twinkling like they often did, making promises I knew Tom was very good at keeping.

Tom's forehead furrowed with curiosity. He brushed his blond bangs from his forehead and shot me a crooked smile. Like magic, deep dimples appeared on either side of his lean, handsome face.

"I like *you*, Val," he teased. "Does *that* count?"

I crinkled my nose and punched him on the arm.

"Ha ha. Very funny." I grabbed Tom's hand and pulled him inside. "Come in for a minute. I want you to try something."

"Sure, I'm up for anything," he teased.

I fished around in the refrigerator and pulled out a rectangular lump swaddled in plastic wrap. I dropped it on the counter with a thud.

"What is that? A brick?" Tom asked.

"Fruitcake. I've been working on the recipe."

I unwrapped the parcel to reveal a golden-brown cake the size and shape of a meatloaf. I cut a ragged slice from the end of it with a bread knife. The jagged chunk was yellow on the inside and dotted with artificial-looking red, green, brown and yellow candied fruit. On closer inspection, it reminded me of the plastic barf I'd once bought from Spencer's as a kid. I plopped the slice on a plate and handed it to Tom.

"Here. Try this."

Tom curled his lip as he broke off a small piece. "Hope it tastes better than it looks." He resigned himself to his fate and popped the chunk in his mouth. He chewed once and his eyebrows rose an inch. "Whoa!"

I grimaced. "That bad?"

Tom shook his head. "No. Pretty good, actually. For *fruitcake*, I mean. But don't give any to Jorge. He'd be officially off the wagon."

I laughed. "Yeah. I think it's gotta be about a hundred proof by now." I reached inside the cupboard. "I've been marinating it for two weeks with this." I held up the bottle of spiced rum.

"Well, that explains it," Tom said. He pushed the plate away.

"You don't want it?" I asked.

Tom smirked. "If I take another bite, you're going to have to drive."

"Fair enough," I laughed. "Let me get my purse."

"Feel like Chinese tonight?" Tom called after me as I padded down the hall to my bedroom.

"Sure. Why not?"

I grabbed my purse from the bed and tugged at the flimsy, tiger-print underwear creeping up my butt. When I turned around, Tom was standing in the doorway. I blushed. He shot me a sexy grin.

"Or, if you prefer, we could have something delivered to your cage, Tiger Lady...."

I was so used to Tom's bad jokes they had become part of his charm. I dropped my purse back on the bed. Tom took me in his arms and kissed me hard on the lips. My back arched all on its own as he nibbled his way down my neck. I kicked off my work heels and forgot all about the fruitcake – I was too busy unbuttoning my blouse.

The doorbell rang. We both froze.

"Who could that be?" Tom asked, his hot breath tickling my ear.

"I have no idea."

"Don't answer it," he whispered.

The bell rang again. Then again.

"It's probably just Laverne," I said. "Wait here. I'll get rid of her."

I fumbled down the hallway, re-buttoning my blouse as I went. When I stuck my eye on the peephole, my mouth fell open.

Standing in the doorway was a woman I, for the most part, only knew about through gossip. She was a familiar stranger to me, like a tabloid personality. I'd both hated and admired her from afar for nearly half a century. She rang the doorbell again and rolled her eyes.

I bit my lip and opened the door.

"Hiya, cuz," she said.

Chapter Four

IT MIGHT'VE JUST BEEN a redneck thing, but when I was growing up a "family vacation" meant piling into a rundown station wagon and driving to a relative's house, hopefully with no more than one breakdown along the way. Once we'd arrived, we'd hang around like useless leeches until either our father's time off work ran out or somebody's patience did. It was almost always the latter. Within a few days, some "misunderstanding" with the host relation and my mother usually had us Jolly clan packing lickety-split and on our way elsewhere.

What went around came around. I was the grown up now, and the bird-brain relatives had come home to roost at *my* place. It's not like my next-door neighbor, Laverne, hadn't warned me. She'd told me that having a house near the beach was akin to holding a winning lottery ticket. It was inevitable that every weird relative I ever knew – and some I'd never heard of – would at some point come crawling out of the woodwork and want to be my new best friend...at least for as long as their vacation days held out.

Lucky me.

I stood at my front door and stared at the first relation to arrive and stake a claim. Dressed in a too-short denim skirt, white t-shirt torn to fringe six inches from the bottom, red cowboy boots and a matching crimson Stetson, this mess of a midlife crisis could have been on her way to shoot the thirtieth-year reunion of *Coyote Ugly*. But no, she'd decided to bless *me* with her presence instead.

I took a quick glance around my front yard. For a split-second, I wondered if my friend Cold Cuts had put her up to this. Nope. No such luck.

"Tammy Jeeter. What are you doing here?"

"I had a week off. Wanted to see how my city-slicker cuz was doin'."

I hadn't gotten so much as a phone call from Tammy in a quarter century. Sure, we'd kept up to date on each other's major victories and defeats through the family grapevine. But on my end, that had meant my mother's version of events. I'd learned long ago any information Lucille Jolly shared with me arrived tainted with more than a touch of sour grapes.

But the information did, nonetheless, *arrive*. I sighed. For once I could actually take comfort in the fact that my mother lived to spread the family gossip. This meant I could reasonably assume that Tammy Jeeter wasn't pregnant, recently escaped from a psycho ward, or on the lam from the law. Lucille Jolly was incapable of withholding news *that* juicy for more than thirty seconds.

From the doorway, I eyed Tammy up and down, unsure what to say to a woman I'd last seen when I wore a size six.

"Hi. I'm Tom Foreman. Val's boyfriend."

Tom's strong, husky voice took me by surprise as it sounded from behind. But I didn't turn around to introduce him properly. I was too aghast at the way Tammy was leering at him. She stepped forward, forcing me to turn sideways between them. Then she cocked her head and her right hip like a loaded, Saturday-night floozy.

"Well, look at you, handsome devil! Nice to meet you, Mr. Tom Foreman."

"Likewise," Tom said without enthusiasm.

Tammy held her hand out to be kissed. Tom smirked and shook her manicured paw instead. "Excuse me," he uttered. "I'll let you two catch up."

Tom let go of Tammy's hand and ambled over to the kitchen. I watched Tammy ogle Tom as he plopped down on a stool, put his elbows on the counter and rested his chin in his hands. He eyed the piece of cake we'd abandoned moments before my cousin's unannounced visit had rendered our bedroom rendezvous null and void.

"Fruitcake," he said sarcastically.

Tammy turned to me, angry-faced. She poked my arm hard. "Have you been talking bad about me, cuz?"

"What?"

Tammy scratched her bleach-blonde scalp with a navy-blue, press-on nail. "Did he just call me a *fruitcake?*"

"Huh? Oh! No...Tom...he just...offered you some *cake.*" I raised my voice. "Right, Tom?"

"What?" Tom looked up, confused. Tammy eyed him with suspicion.

I sighed. "So, look, Tammy, where are you staying?"

An artificial smile sweetened her thin, hard face. "No need to give up your bed, cuz. The couch is fine with me."

Tammy tilted her head, looked past me, and spoke over my shoulder in a voice syrupy enough to induce a diabetic coma. "Oh, Tom, honey? Could you please help me, sugar? My suitcases are in the car."

Tom's sea-green eyes locked on mine, awaiting instructions. I pursed my lips and gave him an infinitesimal nod. He sighed, let go of his grudge about our interrupted evening, and forced a smile. "Sure. Be glad to."

Tammy held up and shook a jumble of keys on a keyring adorned with an insipid, fuzzy white unicorn jumping over a rainbow. "You're a real sweetheart, Tommy! They're in the trunk."

The way Tammy watched Tom walk out the door made me wish I had a lock on his belt buckle. She turned and curled her thin, upper lip. "Nice work, Valiant."

"What do you mean?"

"He's *hot*."

I pretended not to notice. "Oh. Tom? Well...."

"Better watch out!" she cackled.

My eyebrows met halfway up my forehead.

"Just kidding," Tammy backpedaled. "Got any more like him around here?"

"I thought you were with that guy...*Tater Johnson*."

"Heck, no, Valiant. I dumped that cheatin' rascal over three months ago."

"Oh. I didn't know. Sorry about that."

"*I'm* not." Tammy's eyes narrowed and her thin, red lips twisted to one side like a potential serial killer. "Anyway, I had my sights set on your ex, Ricky. But your sister done beat me to him."

Tammy's gut-stab hit its mark. And hard.

"Annie's dating Ricky?" I wheezed.

Tammy looked as innocent as a mail-order bride. "Oh. I thought you *knew*."

"Mom never mentioned it."

Tammy snickered. "I don't doubt it. I'm sure Aunt Lucille was saving that bomb so she could see your face when she dropped it on you."

The fact that Tammy was probably right did nothing to endear her to me. I was scrambling for what to say next when Tom came back inside and saved me the trouble. He shuffled through the front door carrying two butter-yellow suitcases from Sears. I recognized the brand because the Jolly family had graciously bestowed an identical set on *me*, too, right after high-school graduation thirty years ago.

"Where do you want these?" Tom asked me.

"In the second bedroom, please," I answered sweetly.

Tom and I exchanged knowing smiles. The mattress in the second bedroom was a castoff from a buddy of Tom's. It was as lumpy as month-old oatmeal and sagged in the middle like a rubber canoe in a lava pool. Tom's friend couldn't understand why on earth I'd thought the castoff bed had been worth salvaging. "It's horrible," he'd argued. "No one could possibly stand to sleep on it the whole night." But as they say, one man's trash is another man's treasure. For my intents and purposes, the old mattress's flaws were its assets. I didn't care for house guests.

Tom disappeared down the hallway, lugging the scuffed, old luggage. Tammy tossed her purse on the couch and sauntered over to the slice of cake on the counter.

"So, this your fruitcake?"

"Yeah."

She broke off a nibble and chewed it, smacking her red lips annoyingly. "Not bad, Valiant. But I don't think it's got a frog leg's chance in France of winning against your mom's."

"Winning what?" Tom asked as he returned from his new job as Tammy's porter.

"The family fruitcake competition, sugar," Tammy cooed. She smiled at Tom and batted long, spidery eyelashes so thick with mascara they could have induced arachnophobia.

Tom didn't seem to notice. He raised an eyebrow at me. "Family fruitcake competition?"

"It's an old family tradition," Tammy replied before I could answer. "The Family Fruitcake Frenzy." She grinned at me with sadistic pleasure. "Valiant ain't told you about it?"

I winced and took Tom by the hand. Familial pride and shame clashed and jostled about in my heart. Like oil and water, there was simply no way to make them blend.

"It's kind of like the feud between the Hatfields and McCoys," I explained. "Only, instead of shotguns, we use fruitcakes."

Chapter Five

MY COUSIN TAMMY'S UNEXPECTED arrival had left me no choice but to invite her along on my Friday-night date with Tom. Besides, I'd thought it would be fun. We could catch up on all the Jolly family's latest triumphs and catastrophes, and laugh our butts off.

But I'd been wrong. Dead wrong. The whole evening Tammy acted like a hellish crossbreed between a spoiled brat and a jaded nymphomaniac.

At the Chinese restaurant, every word out of my cousin's cruel mouth was a complaint or an insult. "The seats are uncomfortable. The décor is shabby. The waiter is stupid." When our food arrived, sullen Tammy picked at her plate of beef and broccoli, saying "It tastes funny."

The only thing that appeared up to snuff with Tammy's refined redneck standards was the syrupy-sweet plum wine. She'd downed three glasses of it before I could say chicken chow mien. That's when she started to go nympho. Make that super-picky nympho. Between gulps of plum wine, the bitter, blonde country girl threw every man in the restaurant into the wood-chipper. "He's too fat to get laid. He's too old to get it up. He's weird looking – probably some kind of sex offender."

It wasn't long before Tammy had dished out a plateful of ugly that had me questioning my *own* man-griping sessions with Milly. Then I realized there was a difference. Nothing that came out of Tammy's mouth was even remotely funny. Compared to Tammy's bitter, hateful monologue, Milly's and my grousing over men came off like a sketch from *Saturday Night Live.*

No matter how Tom and I tried to steer the conversation, Tammy commandeered it and ran it headlong into a trash pile. After a while, we gave up, bit our lips and resigned ourselves to our fate. I was burning with annoyance and embarrassment. Tom was silent and squirming in his seat like the only rooster left in a coop full of capons. I couldn't blame him. Tammy's non-stop man-bashing could have shriveled *James Bond's* nut-sack to molecular proportions.

On the ride home, Tammy expanded her repertoire of perturbing antics to include kicking the back of my seat over and over. Every time we passed a beach bar, snockered Tammy screeched, "Is *that* where all the *good men* hang out?" When we finally pulled into my driveway, to say I dreaded the fact Tammy was staying the night would have been an understatement on par with, "The sun is warm."

Crap on a cracker! My weekend with Tom was officially toast, and Tammy was a rotten egg.

"So, what are we going to do now?" Tammy whined as Tom shut off the engine to his SUV. I glanced over at him. He stared straight ahead, his mood unreadable.

"I think we're going to call it a night," I said. I reached over the seat and handed Tammy the house keys. "Why don't you go on in, Tammy. I'll be there in a minute."

"I want to go out and party," Tammy complained. "How far is the closest beach bar from here?"

I turned around and stared into her scowling face. "Tammy, if you don't mind, I want to say goodnight to Tom."

"So? Say goodnight, then," she said with the sullen face and crossed arms of an angry child.

"I meant *in private.*"

Tammy kicked my seat for good measure. "Oh. I get it. *Excuuuse me.*" She climbed out of the car, boot-stomped to the front door and went inside. A second later, I saw the blinds rustle. A pair of eyes peered out between the slits.

"Geeze, Tom! What am I gonna do? She's only been here *two hours!* I don't know how much more I can take!"

Tom blew out a huge sigh. "That woman is a piece of work, all right. I'll admit it, Val, I don't envy you one bit."

"Gawd. It feels like she's been here *a year* already."

"Yeah. Well, at least you don't have any balls for her to bust."

I winced. "Sorry about all that."

Tom shrugged. "Not your fault. Anyway, she might be nervous or drunk or something. Give her a little time to adjust."

Gnawing dread mixed with anger in my gut. I pouted. "I don't *want* to, Tom. I want her to go away. *Now.*" I glanced over at the front window. The blinds clicked shut. "Why do you think she's *here*, anyway?"

Tom scrunched his eyebrows into a triangle. "I dunno. To see *you?*"

I shook my head. "I doubt it. I mean, to just drop in like that? Out of the blue? She's got to be up to something."

"Why do you say that?"

"Just a feeling."

Tom pulled me close to him and managed a boyish grin. "Women's intuition?"

I curled my lip. "More like survival instinct."

Tom laughed and kissed me on my crinkled nose. "You're definitely a survivor, Val. No worries on that score."

I blew out a disappointed sigh. "Sorry about fouling up our plans tonight."

"Stop apologizing. You didn't foul anything up. 'Tantalizing Tammy' did."

I jerked away from Tom. "You find her *tantalizing?*"

"I'm a cop. I'm a sucker for a good crime case," he said teased.

I wasn't in the mood for games. "I don't get the joke, Tom. What's Tammy's crime?"

Tom shot me a sideways grin and waggled his eyebrows. "Fishing on private property."

Something clicked in my brain that made my temper flare. "Wait a second. You don't think I'm *jealous* of *Tammy* do you?"

Tom grinned. "Come on, Val! How could you think that?" He shook his head. "You know, you're pathetic when it comes to reading between the lines. I just told you I'm yours. Your *private property*. Get it?"

I did then.

I scooted next to Tom and touched my hand to his cheek. "So *you're* my *private property*, hey?"

Tom took my hand in his and kissed me tenderly on the lips. "Absolutely, Val. And I'd like to think that *you're* mine."

AFTER AN R-RATED MAKE-out session in Tom's SUV, I drug myself back inside to discover Tammy had transformed my home into a redneck sorority house. Sprawled out on my new couch in nothing but her shredded t-shirt and thong underwear, Tammy was guzzling a beer and munching on the last slice of my favorite leftover pizza. There wasn't a napkin or coaster or butt towel in sight.

"So how long you been seeing him?" she asked as I locked the door behind me.

I tried not to bite through my own tongue. "A little over a year."

Tammy whistled. "That's a long time, Val. Are you expecting for Christmas?"

"What?" The woman was on my last nerve. "I'm not *pregnant*, if that's what you mean."

Tammy shook her head and eyed me as if I were pathetic. "No, doofus. A ring. Are you expecting an engagement ring for Christmas? To make it official?"

Up until that very second, no such thought had even remotely crossed my mind. But after Tammy Jeeter planted that insidious little seed in my brain, I couldn't stop watering it. As I lay in bed that night with my eyes wide open, my thoughts sped down two diverging roads like twin, runaway monster trucks.

Did I want that little seed to sprout? Or did I want it to drown?

Chapter Six

I DREAMED I WAS HIKING in the forest with Tom. We strolled, hand in hand, along a winding path of magnificent redwoods. A mountain vista peered at us between the tree limbs. A cool breeze tickled my face. The ground was a soft, spongy pad of reddish-brown pine needles. We came upon a rusty metal sign nailed to a tree. It read; Private Property. Keep Out. Tom tugged on my arm, pulling me toward the tree. I yanked loose of his grip and ran a few steps, but a loud noise made me stop and turn around. Tom was ripping through the sign with a chainsaw....

I awoke with a jolt. My left hand fumbled in the sheets for Tom. He wasn't there. A horrid, deafening noise resonated from the hallway. It sounded like a death match was underway between a roaring lion and an asthmatic bear. A flood of memories washed over me.

Tom isn't here. Tammy Jeeter *is.*

From the sound of it, the ball-busting woman was no *Princess and the Pea*. Despite the dilapidated mattress, Tammy was snoring loud enough to resurrect roadkill.

I sat up and sighed. *Maybe Tom is right. Maybe she'll be different today.*

I drug myself out of bed and brewed a cappuccino, then put on a pot of coffee for 'Tantalizing Tammy.' I had no idea if Tammy drank coffee or not, but I figured I'd at least *try* to be a charitable hostess.

One glance over at the trashed living room made me rescind my charitable offer.

I'd gone to bed last night and left Tammy sprawled on the couch, checking out MatchMate men on her cellphone. She'd gone to bed and left me her freaking mess to clean up. I picked up the pizza box from the coffee table. Beside it was a white ring from a beer bottle, which was now lying on its side in a puddle on the floor. *Great.* I picked up the magazine tossed on my new couch. Underneath it was a greasy pizza sauce smear. Like the Grinch's heart at Christmas, Tammy's rasping snore suddenly grew fifty times more annoying.

Arrgh! Who the hell did she think I was? Her freaking maid?

I marched into my bedroom, yanked a sundress over my head and pulled my hair into a ponytail. Back in the kitchen, I grabbed my cappuccino and stomped off into the backyard. I hoped there I could escape the reaches of Tammy's irritating, rasping existence.

I'D JUST SETTLED INTO a lounge chair by the fire pit when I heard my next-door neighbor call my name. *Crap on a cracker.* I'd wanted some time to myself. The last thing I needed at the moment was more company.

"Mornin', Val!" said a voice too cheery for this early hour.

"Hey, Laverne," I grunted.

"See you've got a visitor. Family?"

"Yes. A cousin. Once removed," I grumbled.

"What does that mean?"

I sighed. "It means I hope to have some peace, once she's removed."

Laverne laughed. "Why is it relatives seem to spoil faster than sushi in the sunshine?"

I looked over and cracked a reluctant smile. Long-legged Laverne was wearing her favorite, gold-thong bikini. Stretched out in a beach lounger, her leathery, 70-something-year-old shriveled butt cheeks were soaking up the glorious rays of the morning sun.

"That's a good question, Laverne. Why *is* it that relatives make the worst house guests?"

Laverne sat up and shrugged her thin, brown shoulders. She ran a liver-spotted hand through her strawberry-blonde curls. "Family comes with a sense of entitlement, I guess. They know you *have* to take 'em in, no matter what."

I heard the sliding glass door roll open. Tammy stuck her squinty-eyed, frizzy haired head out and yelled, "What's for breakfast?"

"There's coffee in the pot," I called back. "Grab yourself a cup."

The sliding glass door closed again with a bang. My blood pressure ticked up twenty points.

"Laverne, she's been here one night and I'm already plotting her murder."

The whites of Laverne's eyes doubled. "My word, sugar!"

"She's hitting on Tom," I grumbled. "She's wrecking my house. She's rude to everybody. And she expects me to wait on her hand and foot. I hate to say it, but she might be worse than my mother!"

Laverne cocked her horsey head and smiled with sympathy. "Well, she *is* on vacation, honey."

"Huh?"

"Hey, aren't you going up to visit your mom for Christmas?"

I scowled. "Yes."

"When are you leaving?"

"Six days, twenty-one hours and thirty-odd minutes from now."

Laverne scratched her head and smiled. "Can't wait, huh?"

I sneered. "Something like that."

"Listen, before you take off, I'd like to have you and Tom over for a nice, holiday dinner. The guys, too. Could you make it this coming Thursday or Friday?"

"Sure. What have you got planned?"

Laverne beamed her perfect, horsey dentures at me. "Turkey and all the trimmings! I want to show off what I learned at my culinary class."

A vision of the last time I'd eaten Laverne's cooking popped into my mind. *A Skinny Dip frozen entrée, still in its paper carton, circled aimlessly in a microwave until it started to blacken and smolder....*

Oh boy. This is going to be awesome. "What can I bring?"

"Nothing, honey," Laverne said. A hint of worry crossed her brow. "Unless you want to bring dessert or something?"

I smiled and took the last sip of my cappuccino. "Okay. I can do that. I'll talk to Tom and get back with you about which day works best. Is that okay?"

Laverne grinned like a Publisher's Clearing House winner. "That sounds great, honey!"

Something crashed inside my house. Laverne's grin faded to a grimace – probably inspired by my own.

"I guess I better go see about that," I said.

I'm not sure how she'd managed it, but in the two minutes since her head had peeked out the back door, Tammy had trashed my kitchen. Coffee and sugar were strewn all over the counter top and floor. The silverware drawer was open, and the carton of milk was left out to sour next to the fridge. A trail of brown coffee drips led away from the scene of the crime, down the hallway and to the closed door of the second bedroom. I nearly lost it.

What an ungrateful freaking slob!

I took a deep breath and tried to regain my composure, then rapped lightly on the door to the guest bedroom. "Tammy? Are you up?"

The gruff voice of a non-morning person barked at me. "Yeah. What are you gonna do about breakfast?"

I love you, too, cousin. "Get dressed. We're going out."

I WAS RELIEVED TO SEE the old blue van in the parking lot of Davie's Donuts as we pulled up. I figured if I was going to have to do battle with my cousin Tammy, I might as well do it on friendly territory, and with reinforcements.

"Hey, Val Pal!" Winky grinned and hollered at me from his shiny chrome stool at the old-fashioned dining counter. I never thought I'd be so grateful to hear his countrified twang.

"Hi, Winky. Good to see you! This is my cousin, Tammy Jeeter."

I held the door open for Queen Tammy to make her royal entrance. She turned her nose up at me as she picked her way inside.

Winky smiled, revealing his lack of dental insurance. "Well, howdy, Miss Tammy. Pleased to meet you."

Like a dime-store mood ring, Tammy's ungrateful glower at me switched to a simpering smile for Winky. She clomped toward my freckled, pot-bellied friend in her shin-high red boots. Her sagging, middle-aged butt cheeks hung out the bottom of her cut-off denim short-shorts like deflated, flesh-colored balloons. I stared in shock as Tammy sidled up to Winky like a two-bit prostitute. She removed her sunglasses with dramatic flair and held out a limp hand for Winky to kiss.

What the hell is up with the hand kissing? Something on reality TV I don't know about?

I guess Winky didn't get it either. He swiveled his chubby torso around on his stool until his back was to us. A second later, he twirled around to face us again. In his chubby, freckled paw was a plate of assorted donut pieces. He held the plate out toward Tammy and gave a gracious, hillbilly nod.

"Care for a donut, Miss Tammy?" he asked.

I recognized the donut chunks as the handy work of Winky's girlfriend, Winnie. As head waitress at Davie's Donuts, she had the wait staff save all customers' uneaten donut parts for "recycling." She'd explained it in all seriousness to me one morning over coffee. "Val, there's no use wasting perfectly good donut remains when I've got a hungry boyfriend to feed."

I opened my mouth to warn Tammy about the pedigree of the secondhand sweets, but before I could say a word, she'd already grabbed the plate.

"Don't mind if I *do*, Winky," Tammy said. She crinkled her turned up nose at me. "You know, I was just about to *starve*." Tammy popped a chunk of slightly-used powdered donut into her impudent maw.

Something inside me did a little happy dance.

Tammy turned her back on me, as if to erase my existence. She climbed onto the stool next to ginger-haired Winky. "Why aren't you the sweetest, most thoughtful man in the world!" she purred, in the way I figured a wayward waif in a cheap romance novel would. I smiled as Tammy popped a chunk of cruller in her mouth. But when she leaned over and gave Winky a gander at her goose eggs, I was caught off guard.

As I stood frozen in disgust, a blissfully unaware Winnie emerged from behind the kitchen door with a pot of coffee. Tammy whistled at her like she was a dog.

"Hey, you. *Waitress*. Cup of coffee here."

Plump, black-haired Winnie squinted at Tammy through her red-framed glasses. She turned toward me and smiled in recognition. "Oh. Hi, Val!"

"I meant *now*," Tammy demanded.

Winnie pursed her lips, then walked over to Tammy and poured her a cup.

"Is that *decaf*?" Tammy snarled.

"Um. No," Winnie fumbled. "It's regular."

"I said *decaf*. Can't you hear?"

Every fiber in my being wanted to bitch-slap Tammy right then and there. But for the moment, I decided to settle for an apologetic smile aimed in Winnie's direction.

"Winnie, I want you to meet my cousin Tammy. Tammy, this is Winnie, *Winky's girlfriend*," I said with all the cheer I could muster. "I'll take that cup of regular, Winnie."

I plucked the mug of coffee from the counter in front of Tammy and took a sip, all the while shooting Tammy the evil eye. I turned to Winnie and smiled like a hundred-watt bulb. "Thanks, Winnie." I set my coffee down in front of the empty stool next to my cousin. "I'll be back in a minute. I'm going to the ladies' room."

I didn't need to pee. I needed to chill out. And vent. And figure out a way to gracefully ditch that hideous hillbilly from hell. I marched to the bathroom, closed the door behind me and punched Milly's number on my cellphone.

"Milly? My cousin is a two-faced skank!"

"Who is this?"

"It's *me. Val.*"

"Geeze! You sound like you're in a tunnel. What are you talking about?"

"My cousin Tammy. She showed up on my doorstep last night. She's horrible!"

"What's she doing at your place? Where'd she come from?"

"I don't know. *Satan spawn*, maybe?"

The bathroom door flew open. Winnie bustled in, red-faced and out of breath.

"Val! Quick! You've got to come help me!" she wheezed.

"Hold on, Milly," I said into the phone. "I might need to call you back."

Poor Winnie looked ready to burst. Whether it was into flames or tears, I couldn't tell for sure. "What's wrong, Winnie?"

"It's your cousin Tammy!" she bellowed. "That tramp's all over Winky like a piranha on a corndog!"

Chapter Seven

"WHAT DO YOU CALL THESE again?" Tammy slurred. She sucked on a straw until her cheeks caved in. Loud slurping sounds emanated from the bottom of her pineapple-shaped glass.

"Sex on the beach," I answered for the third time.

Tammy laughed, then burped, then laughed even louder. "Ha ha! I *know* that. I just like to make you say it."

I'd lured Tammy away from Davie's Donuts with the promise of cocktails on the beach. Winnie had been grateful, even if Tammy had not. I glanced at my cellphone.

Good grief. It was barely noon.

Seven long hours of babysitting brat-nympho Tammy still loomed before I could escape with Tom and my friends for dinner tonight. Time hadn't stood this still for humankind since the Paleozoic Era.

I wracked my brain for something to talk about with my cousin, but came up empty. Tammy's only apparent interests were men and alcohol. Thought I enjoyed the two myself, our tastes in both couldn't have been more diametrically opposed. She had an eye for scruffy, bearded bikers and booze hounds. And she drank – ugh – sweet, fruity cocktails with paper umbrellas in unnatural colors that glowed in the dark.

I sighed and glanced around the soulless tourist trap called Barnacle Bill's. Mass-produced beach "memorabilia" plastered its obscenely orange walls. A purple, plastic octopus held up a sign that read, "Free

Beer Yesterday." One look around the bar made me realize *I* was the actual oddball here. I had on age-appropriate clothes and was stone-cold sober. Everyone else, including Tammy, had put their desperation on display by drinking too much and wearing too little. Poor souls. They were probably trying to make up for a lifetime of doing the opposite.

I'd taken Tammy to Barnacle Bill's "Disneyland for Drunks" to avoid desecrating my *real* favorite beach haunts. Still, when my snockered cousin started bellowing *99 Bottles of Beer on the Wall*, I was forced to put my foot down, even there.

"Might want to slow it down a bit with the booze, Tammy."

"Why? I'm on vacation!" she said indignantly, as if that justified anything and everything.

If I'd had a drink myself, I might have found her comment amusing. But I hadn't dared. I was the designated driver. Besides, it was hard enough to keep from slapping Tammy when I had full control of all my faculties.

I forced a smile. "It's noon. How about some lunch?"

Tammy toyed with her straw and pouted with suspicion. "What do they have here?"

"Oh, no, Tammy. Not *here*. I know a *much* better place. Come on. Let's go."

I drug Tammy off her barstool and helped her stumble through the parking lot to my car. By the time we made it home, she'd lost her shoes and was almost comatose. I held her floppy torso up as she lurched and hobbled into the house. We'd just made it to the second bedroom before she collapsed onto the lumpy mattress. I turned her on her side and covered her with a blanket. Before I could step into the hall, Tammy was sawing logs like an industrial band saw.

I returned and put a bucket by her bedside, and checked in on her throughout the afternoon. When it appeared that she was going to survive, I jumped in the shower, got dressed and put on a touch of makeup. I wrote Tammy a note reminding her of my date with Tom and set it on the kitchen counter next to a glass of water and a couple of aspirin. I cut the volume on my cellphone and set it to vibrate, then texted Tom.

"Text me when you're almost here."

"Okay," came his quick reply.

I didn't have much in the fridge, so I set a couple of delivery menus from nearby restaurants on the counter next to the note. I was giving my face one last check in the mirror when I felt my phone vibrate. It was another text from Tom. "Here."

I tucked my phone in my purse and glanced around like a teenage runaway. The coast was clear. I picked up my purse and shoes, and tip-toed barefoot across the living room and out the front door. Once outside, I turned the deadbolt key as slow as molasses, so as not to make a sound. When Tom pulled up behind me and tooted his horn as a joke, I about jumped out of my skin. I slipped into my sandals and bolted for his SUV.

"Hey there, good-looking," Tom said in his slow, charming drawl.

"Hey!" I grunted as I scrambled into the passenger seat. I gave Tom a peck on the lips, then shot a worried glanced back at the house. I thought I saw the blinds in the second bedroom move. If a bloody guy in a hockey mask had appeared in the window, it wouldn't have terrified me more.

"Hit the gas, Tom! Let's get the hell out of here!"

"What? Why?"

"Go! Now! Just do it!"

Tom shifted into reverse and peeled out. "Geeze! What's gotten into you, Val?"

"Let's just say I've got a bad case of the 'Jeeters.'"

WOW. WHAT A DIFFERENCE the right company could make.

From our vantage point at a table on the wooden deck at Jimmy D's Beach Bar, the sunset over the Gulf of Mexico was spectacular. The pink sky tinted everyone's face with a sweet, rosy glow. A warm breeze blew my hair around and tickled my face like a frizzy feather. I smiled and breathed a giddy sigh of relief.

"As corny as it sounds, we live in paradise," Vance said. He smiled at Milly, then raised his beer bottle to make a toast.

"We truly do," Milly agreed. She raised her beer and returned his goofy smile.

"To paradise," Vance said.

"To paradise," Tom and I chimed in.

Milly and Vance had been dating for four months, and were in that google-eyed phase of a fresh, new romance. Blonde, fair-skinned, and wearing a white sundress, Milly looked like a ghost compared to tan, dark-haired Vance. Like a pair of kitschy salt-and-pepper shakers, the two looked so shiny and happy and hopeful it almost made me hurt inside. I remembered feeling that way, too. But as of late, it seemed all I could do was complain.

Vance kissed Milly. I looked over at Tom. He squeezed my hand and smiled at me in a soft, easy way that made my stomach relax. *What on earth did I have to complain about?*

Still, the compulsion overtook me.

"I've been held hostage all day in hillbilly hell," I blurted.

Milly's left eyebrow shot up. "Well, it's Saturday, so I know you're not talking about me or Griffith & Maas," she quipped.

Her response wasn't what I'd been fishing for. After a whole day of trying to keep tabs on my hard-drinking, country cousin, I was in dire need of a sympathetic ear.

"I'm talking about *Tammy*," I said. "Geeze, Louise. Today was *awful*. I feel like I'm being punished for some horrible crime I didn't commit."

Milly shrugged. "What do you want *us* to do about it, Val? If you don't like her company, tell her to leave."

I scowled. "You've met my family, Milly. It's not that easy."

"Wait a minute," Tom interjected. He locked eyes with Milly. "You've met Val's family?"

Milly shrugged. "Not everyone. Her mom. Stepdad. Couple of aunts and uncles."

"I didn't know that," Tom said.

"That's why I was talking to Milly about it," I whined. "She understands. Milly, my cousin is a two-timing twit."

Milly laughed. "I haven't had the pleasure, but I'll take your word for it."

"I can corroborate her observation," Tom said in his cop voice.

Vance laughed. "Sounds like there's a story behind that remark."

Tom shook his head. "Don't ask."

"Believe me, Tom," Milly said, "no matter how bad Tammy is, she's merely a little sample of what you have in store." She smirked and raised her beer to make a toast. "Happy holidays!"

A crowd of people at the bar cheered, as if in response to Milly's toast.

"Looks like someone scored," Vance said to Milly. "Mind if I go check on the game? I'll just be a minute."

Milly gave him the googly eyes again. "Not at all."

"I think I'll go with him," Tom said. "Stretch my legs."

After the two men left, I ambushed my poor, unsuspecting friend.

"Geeze, Milly! Tammy's the Jekyll and Hyde of Greenville! What was I thinking? I actually used to think of her as a role model!"

Milly stared at me like I was crazy. "What are you talking about?"

I hung my head. "I never told anyone, but Tammy was a big reason why I left Jimmy Johnson. Believe it or not, I thought she knew the secret to having a happy life."

"What?" Milly looked horrified.

I shook my head. "I know. But ever since she was a kid, Tammy's always done as she darn well pleased. Ugh! She still does! The thing is, Milly, I thought Tammy *was right*. I was miserable with Jimmy, for sure. So I followed her example. I ditched him without really thinking it through."

"Val, it was time to leave Jimmy. Don't beat yourself up on that score."

I smiled at Milly. "Thanks. But here's the thing. What I didn't realize until today was the *path of destruction* Tammy leaves in her wake. I wonder...have I done the same thing?"

Milly reached across the table and grabbed my hand. "Are you kidding? Look, Val. We all dream of starting over once in a while. And sometimes, letting things go is the right thing to do. And by things I mean *people*, too – like Jimmy. I mean, who knows? Nobody's perfect. And not all things are meant to last a lifetime."

I sighed with relief. "Thanks for not judging me too harshly."

"We all make mistakes, Val. Some of us learn from them. Others repeat the same ones over and over, like gerbils on a wheel."

I rubbed a hand on my forehead and grimaced. "It took me way too long to get off that wheel, Milly."

Milly smiled. "Hey, at least you're not on it now. For the record, I love you, you know."

The knot in my stomach relaxed. I smiled. "Thanks. I love you, too. Hey, Milly?"

"Yeah?"

"Tom made a joke the other night, but I don't think he was actually joking. He said he wanted us to be each other's 'private property.'"

Milly crinkled her button nose. "What do you mean? Like exclusive? I thought you guys already were."

"Yeah. But I'm not so sure about –"

Milly sat up straight. "Sure about what, Val?" She glanced toward the men at the bar and lowered her voice. "Are you saying you think you can do better than Tom? He's a great guy!"

My eyes widened. "No. I mean....no!" I shook my head softly. "That's not what I mean at all!"

Milly folded her arms across her chest. "Then what *did* you mean?"

"I guess what I'm trying to say is, *I don't want things to change*, Milly. I'm not thinking I could do better than Tom. I'm afraid things could get *worse* between us. A *lot* worse. If we took the next step, I mean."

"The next step?" Milly unfolded her arms and leaned in across the table. "Has Tom *proposed* to you?"

"No! But. I mean, he might."

"And if he does?"

"I don't know. This whole 'living together' thing. It never seems to work out for me. It's like that old saying, familiarity breeds contempt, right?"

Milly laughed. "In your case, I think it's *family* breeds contempt."

"I'm not joking, Milly."

Milly smirked. "Neither am I."

I swallowed a knot in my throat and changed the subject. "So, how are things going with you and Vance?"

Milly's eyes went all googly again.

"SORRY THAT TAMMY ENDED up ruining our weekend, Tom," I said as he drove us back to my place.

Tom offered me a sympathetic smirk. "You know Val, for someone who hates to apologize, you seem to be doing a lot of it lately."

"I'm sorry...." I caught myself and laughed. "How is it that the mere *thought* of some people can make your stomach knot up?"

Tom smiled and touched his hand to my cheek. "It's okay, Val. I've got a few fruitcakes in my family bakery, too."

As Tom pulled up in my driveway, I noticed Tammy's car was gone. My house, however, was lit up like Grand Central Station. My dear cousin had left every bulb I owned burning. Still, I exhaled with relief at the idea she wasn't inside waiting for me.

"Looks like Tammy's not here, Tom. Want to come in? Maybe have a fruitcake nightcap?"

Tom smirked. "Or maybe a nightcap with a fruitcake?"

I punched him on the arm. He laughed. "I guess I could be persuaded to see you to the door."

When I turned the front doorknob, it gave way. Tammy had left it unlocked. *How thoughtful. Geeze! Good thing Tom is with me.*

"Would you mind scouring the place for hidden ax murderers?" I asked. "I'll make you a Tanqueray and tonic for your troubles."

"Always ready to serve," Tom laughed.

As he disappeared down the hallway, I yelled after him. "And turn out some lights along the way!"

I poured gin into two highball glasses and clunked in a few ice cubes. I'd just added the tonic and slices of lime when Tom returned.

"Those look good," he said. "I think it's time for a toast."

We raised our glasses. "To what?" I asked.

"To us, of course," Tom said, and winked at me.

I grinned. "To us."

As the glasses clinked together, I savored the tinkling sound in the blessed silence.

"It's so quiet without Tammy here," I whispered.

"Looks like you can get used to it," Tom said. "It's not just Tammy that's gone. Her ugly suitcases are, too."

Chapter Eight

"CRAP ON A CRACKER!" I yelled.

"Geeze, Val," Tom laughed. "I thought you'd be happy."

I bit my lip. "Tammy's gone, Tom. And I'm...*responsible*."

"Responsible? Says who? From what I've seen, the woman can take care of herself just fine."

I set my gin and tonic down and glanced over at the kitchen counter. "She didn't take the aspirin I left out for her. Hopefully, that means she wasn't sick."

Tom smirked. "She didn't take your stereo, either. I guess we can rule out robbery as a motive for her visit."

"Weird." I crinkled my nose and bared my teeth. "I should feel bad, shouldn't I?"

"Why?"

"I don't know. Guilt's been programmed into my DNA, okay?"

Tom raised an eyebrow and grinned. "I believe *that*."

"Tom, I don't get it. Why the hell did she come here in the first place if she was going to be nothing but a pain in the butt, trash my place, and not even have a civil word to say?"

"As far as I can tell, Tammy was just looking for a free place to crash while she found herself a new guy to castrate." Tom winked and shot me a boyish grin. "Or maybe your merciless mattress scheme worked after all."

I grinned despite myself. "Well, then. Here's to the mattress for a job well done." I raised my glass in the air.

"To the mattress," Tom echoed, and finished his drink.

"Want another?" I asked.

"Yeah. Why not. With Tammy gone, I can finally spend the night."

I opened the fridge to grab another lime from the veggie drawer.

"Tammy took the cake," I said.

"She sure did."

I stood up and turned around. "No, Tom. I mean the fruitcake. She took it."

Tom's eyebrows scrunched together. "Why would she do that?"

I shook my head in wonder. "I have no idea."

"She left the house unlocked," Tom chided. "Maybe a drunk hobo wandered in and stole it."

"Ha ha," I sneered. "Bad theory. If a drunkard took it, he would have stolen the booze, too."

"Good point, Valiant Stranger," Tom joked.

I stuck my superior detective nose in the air and opened the kitchen cabinet to prove my point. My heart skipped a beat. The bottle of spiced rum was missing, too.

"Okay. Now I'm officially worried," I said.

Tom pursed his lips. "I'll give the house another look through, just in case."

WITH MY HOUSE COP-CERTIFIED free of all vagrants, rum and fruitcakes, Tom and I went back to our original weekend plans. After a night of making love, we awoke Sunday morning to the bliss of hitting the snooze button and cappuccinos in bed. I was first to get up that morning, so I brewed us up a batch. I handed Tom his cup and snuggled back into the sheets beside him.

"I could get used to this," he said, and wrapped an arm around me.

I smiled to hide a sudden pang of fear. "Me, too."

"We should decorate your place for the holidays, Val. You've got plenty of room for a Christmas tree."

I scowled. "What for?"

Tom squeezed me playfully. "What for? Is that all the holiday spirit you've got?"

"Yes. Disappointment's destroyed the rest."

Tom laughed. "Come on. Not even a sprig of mistletoe?"

"No," I whined.

Tom set his cup on the nightstand and kissed me on the nose. "Come on. Mistletoe could be fun...."

"Hah! I doubt it," I groused and squirmed away. I always played hard to get on Sunday mornings. It was kind of "our thing."

"Now don't be that way," Tom teased and pulled me back toward him. "Santa sees you when you're grouchy, you know."

"And he sees you when you're sleazy!"

Tom laughed. "Sleazy?" He grabbed my cup and put it on the nightstand beside his. "I'll show you sleazy."

He did.

"SPEAKING OF HOLIDAY disasters, Laverne invited us to dinner," I said. Tom and I were lying tangled up together in the hammock in my backyard, enjoying the beautiful view of the Intracoastal Waterway and the delicious exhaustion of afterglow.

"Who was talking about holiday disasters?" Tom asked.

"Oh. Maybe I was just *thinking* about them."

"Val," Tom sighed, "you've got six more days before we head to your mom's. All this worrying. You're starting to make me have second thoughts about going."

I squirmed up onto an elbow until we were nose-to-nose. "No way are you backing out on me now, mister! I promised my mother. Besides, of all the people I know, you're the only one with a reliable car. Except Milly, of course. And she's refused to ever set foot in Jackson County again."

Tom grimaced. "Why?"

I laid back down beside him and crossed my arms. "I plead the fifth. So, does Thursday or Friday work better for you?"

Tom reached across my arms and took my hand. "I'll take you any day of the week."

I smirked. "I mean for Laverne's dinner party. She gave us the option."

"It'll have to be Friday, Val. We've got my precinct party Thursday, remember?

"Oh, that's right. With all the stuff going on...."

Tom put a pout on his lips and a feminine spin on his voice. "I can't believe it. You forgot all about it, didn't you?"

"I did not! I...had a...temporary memory lapse."

Tom hugged me to him. "Wow. Picture that. Val Fremden getting old and losing it like the rest of us."

I sneered. "I'm still younger than *you*."

Tom grabbed his chest. "And she takes her killer shot."

"Ha ha. So, Friday for Laverne. I'll let her know."

"What have you got planned for the rest of the day, young lady?"

"Apologies."

Tom looked at me sideways. "What?"

"Tammy was awful to Winnie. I want to go by Davie's and apologize."

"I could go for a donut."

I smiled at my handsome cop. "I had a feeling you could."

PULLING OUT OF MY DRIVEWAY in Tom's silver 4Runner, we spotted Winnie's decrepit Dodge van ambling down the road. To my surprise, it pulled into Laverne's driveway instead of mine. The doors flew open and Winky, Jorge and Goober piled out like a chain-gang of incarcerated elves. Each had on a red Santa hat and a bright-green vest. The scene made me think of an idea for a low-budget horror flick. *Santa's Chain Gang of Evildoers.*

"Stop the car," I told Tom needlessly. He already had.

"What the heck are those three up to now?" he asked.

"I dunno. Let's find out."

Tom turned off the engine. We piled out and picked our way across the lawn toward Laverne's place. Elfin-clad Jorge ran over to meet us. The dark-skinned Latino grinned from ear to ear and waved a rolled-up piece of paper at us. He called out to us cheerfully.

"Hola, Val and Tom!"

"Hey, buddy!" Tom called back. "What you got there?"

"It's a drawing." Jorge unrolled the scroll and held it out for us to examine. Etched in black ink was a rough sketch of Laverne's house. On one end of the roof, a Santa-like figure pulled the handle on a slot machine. At the other end, seven reindeer kicked a back leg up and danced the cancan.

"What on earth...?" Tom mumbled.

"It's our new business," Jorge explained. "We're the Three X-migos. We're gonna put up holiday lights for people. Laverne's our first customer!"

"That's pretty cool!" Tom said.

"I wanted to call it HAWG," Winky interjected. "That's short for Horge And Winky, 'n' Goober. But them two voted it down." Winky pouted, then tugged on the bottom hem of his green vest for emphasis.

"Winky," I explained, "Jorge doesn't start with an H."

"It don't?" Winky scratched underneath his Santa cap and spit a stream of brown chew into the grass. "Dang. Now I got to rewrite all my Christmas cards."

Tom took the scroll from Jorge and studied it as the third elf, Goober, approached.

"Wow," Tom said. "This is actually a great idea. Who did the drawings?"

"Yo. I mean, me!" Jorge beamed.

"I love it, Jorge!" I said. "How many customers have you got?"

"Counting Laverne, a grand total of one," Goober deadpanned.

I looked up at my tall, lanky friend. Goober had earned his nickname through the misfortune of having a bald head shaped exactly like a roasted peanut. Standing next to Winky and Jorge, six-foot-tall Goober looked like a stand in for Will Ferrell in *Elf*.

"One customer, huh? Well, you've got to start somewhere," Tom said. "You can do my house, if you want."

"Hot dog!" Winky hollered.

"Watch your language," Jorge warned his freckle-faced colleague. "We're *elves*, now."

Winky pursed his lips and nodded solemnly.

"Why don't you boys look darlin'!" Laverne yelled from her doorstep. "I got a pot of coffee on. Y'all come on in!"

I grabbed Tom by the arm and yelled back at Laverne. "We've got to go by Davie's Donuts. I promised this cop a donut, and I need to apologize to Winnie."

"What for?" Winky asked.

"For my cousin Tammy. She treated her awful."

Winky laughed. "Oh, my old Winnie girl is all right. Sure, she was jealous for a little bit. But she calmed down when I told her I preferred brains over boobs. No disrespect, but that cousin a yore's wern't no inner lectual."

"What?" Tom asked.

I nudged Tom on the arm and shook my head. I scanned the three men's faces capped in red Santa hats and tried not to smirk. "So, who's the genius behind *this* new scheme?"

Goober raised an index finger. "That would be me."

"Where'd you get the idea?"

"Saw a flyer on a light pole. Sounded easier than going back to work for the public school system."

I nodded. "Well, you can't argue with that."

Chapter Nine

IT WAS MONDAY MORNING at Griffith & Maas. Milly and I took a coffee break in her office to swap weekend gossip. I filled her in on all the gory details about my strange visit from Cousin Tammy. I'd tried to put a funny spin on the story, but it seemed to put Milly in a funk instead. She took a sip of coffee and stared blankly out the window.

"I know her type. Never met a woman she wouldn't throw under the bus," Milly said.

"Yeah. *Exactly*," I agreed.

"I used to have a friend kind of like Tammy," Milly explained. "Her name was Karen. She was always ditching me for some new man she'd just met. It took me a while, but one day I finally realized I wasn't her friend. I was just 'Plan B' until someone with a penis came along."

"That sounds like Tammy all right," I agreed. "But unlike Karen, Tammy doesn't like to wait. If no man comes along quick enough, she takes yours. Or she'll try to, at least."

"Come on, Val. Don't make her out to be worse than she already is."

"It's true! I forgot to tell you. The woman tried to steal Winky away from Winnie. And I'm pretty darn sure she took my fruitcake. I was making it for the holidays, you know."

"That's awful. And *weird*." Milly drummed her nails on her desk. "Winky? I guess maybe he's got his redneck charms. But a *fruitcake?*" Milly bit her lip. "Maybe she needed something to nibble on, on her way back to Hooterville."

Milly had renamed Greenville "Hooterville" after our brief visit there together last year. She did it to tease me. But to be honest, it *was* a more accurate moniker.

"I guess," I replied. "If Tammy *did* take my fruitcake, she won't have to worry about it going bad in the car. That cake has enough rum in it to preserve it into the next millennium."

Milly laughed. "Okay. Break's over. Back to work."

I took a step toward Milly's office door, but another thought turned me back around. "Oh. Speaking of food, Laverne's having a dinner party on Friday night. You and Vance are invited."

"Friday?" Milly put on her thinking cap. "I think we have the night free. Should I bring something?"

"Only if you want to eat actual food. Laverne's culinary skills are legendary...and I don't mean that in a good way."

Milly crinkled her nose. "Got 'cha. Will Cold Cuts be there?"

"I don't know. I need to call her. Last time we spoke she was up near Tallahassee shooting a commercial for some politician, I think."

"It'd be great to see her. She's the only person I know who's more abnormal than you."

I shot Milly a smirk. "Gee, thanks."

Milly knitted her eyebrows together, tapped an index finger on her cheek and muttered to herself. "Abnormal...abnormal. Hmmm. That's ringing a bell...." Suddenly her face lit up with a devious grin. She pointed her tapping finger at me like a gun. "Ah yes! Your vacation days have been approved. You're free to visit your dear old mom. With our blessings, of course."

I sneered. "How can I ever thank you?"

Milly smirked like a she-devil. "Hope you have a nice trip, Val. Wish I could come along. *Not.*"

"Milly, I hope all you get for Christmas is a lump of coal in your stocking."

Milly laughed. "If I did, I'd still come out way ahead of you."

WHEN I GOT HOME, THREE sweaty elves were working underneath the hood of Winnie's van at the end of Laverne's driveway. I shifted Maggie into park and went over to investigate.

"What's up?" I asked the trio of male backsides bent over the engine.

Three overgrown dwarves turned around to face me. Greasy, Oily and Sweaty.

"Think it's the timing belt," Winky said. "Ain't got the parts here to fix it."

"Looks like we're stranded," Jorge shrugged.

"You guys need a lift back home?" I asked.

"That'd be right good a you," Winky said.

"Okay. But no Snow White jokes along the way. And no singing, *Hi Ho*."

"Oh, drat," Goober deadpanned. "You spoiled all my plans."

AS I PULLED INTO JORGE'S driveway with the Three X-migos on board, I realized I'd only been there once before. That had been five months ago, shortly after Jorge's mother had gotten married and given him the family homestead. Relocating hadn't been a big move for Jorge. He'd been living in his mother's garage for years. But after she remarried and left, Winky, Goober and Winnie had moved in to keep Jorge company – and to keep him sober. Jorge had remained, for the most part, drunk as a skunk since his wife and kids were killed in an auto accident years ago.

My only prior visit to Jorge's place was back in June. It was a party to celebrate his's 40th day of sobriety. Since then, with the help of his buddies, Jorge had made it past the six-month mark without a drink.

I guess that's why I was surprised to walk in and find the place littered with beer bottles. I picked one up off the floor.

"*This* can't be helpful," I said, and shot Winky and Goober a stern look.

"It's okay, Val," Jorge said. He shrugged. "It's like if I was fat. They couldn't give up eating. Booze is everywhere. I have to get used to it."

Winky shot me a told-you-so sneer and picked up the phone on the kitchen wall and began dialing.

"How do you manage it, Jorge?" I asked.

"It's not so bad. I took up some other hobbies. Like cooking. And drawing. And drinking coffee."

I glanced around the kitchen. There must have been fifty empty coffee cans stacked up around the counter tops. "That's a lot of coffee." I picked up a tin and shook it. It rattled. Coffee doesn't rattle.

"Winnie saves them up for us from Davie's," Goober explained. "I'm starving, Jorge. What's for supper?"

Jorge smiled like a loving mother. "Leftover chicken and rice. You want to stay, Val? We got plenty."

"It's actually pretty good," Goober confessed. "This guy can cook like a pro." Goober put a basketball-player-sized hand on Jorge's shoulder and shook him like guys do.

"Sure," I said. "Why not."

Jorge grinned and hugged me. "Bueno!" He dove into the fridge and pulled out three beat-up metal pots. He banged them onto the heating coils on the stove top, then turned on the knobs with an artful flick of his wrist. "I got a system," he said as he beamed at me with pride.

"Can I help?" I asked.

"Sure!" Jorge pulled open a cabinet door. "We'll use the good stuff tonight."

The melamine plates Jorge handed me were warped and worn at the edges. I recognized the golden wheat pattern from visits to my grandma's as a child. If this was the "good stuff," I didn't want to see the bad stuff.

"Okay, I'll set the table." I carried the dishes to the dining room and hit a snag. The table was already set – with last night's dirty dinner dishes.

"Parts is ordered," Winky said behind me as he hung up the phone. "Oops. Good golly. I think it was my turn to do the dishes last night. My bad." Winky circled the table, stacking up the dirty paper plates and brushing food crumbs onto the stack. "There you go, Val."

I stifled a cringe and set the table with the good stuff.

While Jorge heated up dinner, I took a quick tour of the place. It was a small ranch house like mine, built in the 1950s. But it had a master suite on one end, two bedrooms and a bath on the other. The kitchen and living room were located in the center of the house. I snuck a peek in the master bedroom. Above the bed, high up on the wall, hung a life-sized velvet picture of Rambo shooting a machine gun. A chest of drawers on the opposite wall was covered in a jumble of cheap costume jewelry. I smiled. Jorge had given Winnie and Winky the master suite.

At the other end of the house, one of the bedroom doors was ajar. I stuck my head in and was shocked to see a floral bedspread covering a full-sized bed. Bottles of perfume and family portraits lined the tops of the dresser and chest of drawers. Anyone could have been forgiven for mistaking this for a woman's bedroom. But a closer inspection of the subjects in the pictures told a different tale.

Half of the photos were of Jorge and his buddies during his former glory days on the police force. I recognized a younger-looking Tom in several of them. The other half of the framed photos were Jorge's mother and his wife and kids. They smiled back at me eerily, frozen in time. A twinge pricked my heart. All of a sudden I felt like a voyeur. I backed out Jorge's room and closed the door. Across the hall, the door to the remaining bedroom was shut. A sign tacked to it instructed potential nosy visitors to "Keep Out."

I heeded Goober's warning and wandered into the living room. A somewhat new, overstuffed lounge chair looked radiant as the sun compared to the worn-out, plaid sofa beside it. A peek out the backdoor caught me by surprise. The lawn was neatly trimmed, and flowerbeds lined the wooden privacy fence. A shiny, round Weber barbeque grill took pride of place on the concrete patio. I smiled. *The guys are doing okay.*

When I returned to the kitchen. Jorge had not only heated up dinner – he'd brewed a batch of tea. He poured the hot, brown liquid into red plastic glasses filled with ice.

"You ready to eat?" he asked.

"Sure. Let me carry a couple of those." I grabbed two glasses.

Jorge hollered down the hall past me, "Dinnertime!"

"Okay!" came the voices of Winky and Goober.

A nostalgic feeling fell over me like warm, soft netting. As the four of us sat down to eat, my eyes brimmed with unexpected tears. Goober heaped my plate with chicken and rice and looked at me with the curiosity of a captive primate.

"Come on, Val. Like I said, Jorge's cooking's not that bad."

"What? Oh. It's not the food, Goober." I turned to Jorge and batted back my tears. "This looks absolutely delicious."

"Then what is it?" Goober asked.

I stared down at my plate of chicken and rice. I could feel their eyes on me. "I don't know. It reminds me of...*home*, I guess."

I looked up and tears spilled down my cheeks. All three men smiled back at me. Winky reached across the table and handed me a paper towel.

"None of that, now," he said in a sweet tone I'd never heard before.

I wiped my eyes, sniffed and took a big bite of chicken and rice. It was scrumptious. I gave Jorge a thumbs up and took another mouthful as the guys stared at me like proud parents. I was searching my mind for something stupid to say to ruin the moment when the doorbell rang, shifting the attention off me. I breathed a sigh of relief.

"I'll get it," Goober said. He stood up and headed toward the door.

I took a sip of tea to wash down the food and noticed the ice had melted. "Anybody want more ice?" I asked. Jorge and Winky shook their heads, their mouths full of collard greens and yellow rice.

I padded toward the kitchen, but stopped midway. From this vantage point, I could see Goober as he talked to a mangy-looking guy standing outside the front door. The scrawny, long-haired man handed Goober a black garbage bag. Some money changed hands. Goober gave the fellow a couple of coffee cans. The guy nodded. "Be back in a couple of days," he said.

"Good doing business with you," Goober replied, then shut the door. As he walked toward the dining room, I ambushed him and dragged him into the kitchen.

"Are you dealing drugs, Goober?"

Goober looked aghast. "What? No!"

I exhaled with relief, but kept my eyes locked on Goober. "So what were you doing with that man, then?"

I opened the freezer door and reached inside to get some ice for my tea.

"Legitimate, bonafide business," Goober said.

My hand fell on something unidentifiable in the freezer. I shifted my eyes from Goober to the inside the fridge. My hand was resting on a clear plastic bag lying next to the ice bag. When I lifted my hand, the frozen face of a rat stared back at me with a goofy grin. An involuntary, high-pitched squeal shot out of my mouth.

"Ahhhh!" I slammed the freezer door. My knees buckled beneath me. If Goober hadn't grabbed me I'd have hit the floor.

"What's going on here, Goober? Why are there *rats* in your *freezer?*"

"Don't be so dramatic, Val," Goober said. "Their gerbils. Not rats."

Winky and Jorge came barreling into the kitchen. Winky tried to stop in his stocking feet and ended up crashing into the cabinets. I wrestled myself from Goober's supportive arms.

"What in blue blazes is going on here?" Winky hollered.

"She saw the gerbils," Goober said casually, and shrugged.

"Oh," said Jorge. "The way you screamed, we thought you went and looked in the bathroom or something."

"What?" I stared at the men, stunned and incredulous. "Who...who killed all those gerbils?" My eyes fell on the pot full of chicken and rice. "You're not...*eating* them are you?"

"Gross!" Winky said. "Even *we* got our standards, Val!"

"Get ahold of yourself," Goober said to me. "No pets were harmed in the making of your dinner. But I have to say, that's a pretty hypocritical point of view you're taking. Whether it's a chicken from on a farm or a rat from a pet shop, something died to make your dinner. What's the difference?"

"There's a *big* difference!" I argued.

"Yeah? What?" Goober asked.

I fumbled for an answer. "Chickens don't have...*personalities*, okay?"

"Tell that to my Aunt Carla," Jorge said. "She has chickens. She gave all of them names."

"Like what?" Winky asked.

"Fried, Boiled and Fricasseed," Jorge smirked. The men fell about the place laughing.

"You guys are impossible!" I yelled. "Is anyone going to tell me why you have dead rats in your freezer?"

"I already told you, Val. They're not rats," Goober said. He smoothed his bushy moustache with a thumb and forefinger. "Not all of them, anyway. There's also a couple of gerbils in there." He winked at me. "Not to mention a stew-sized guinea pig named Fred."

Anger finally eclipsed my horror. "For the third time, *why are there members of the rodent family in your freezer?*"

"Economics, Val," Goober said. He pursed his lips and shook his head at me. "It's implausible to rely on hanging holiday lights for ample remuneration year round. It's purely *seasonal* work. Therefore, we've found gainful, steady employment in the groundbreaking field of pet cremation."

"*Ground breakin'!*" Goober hollered. "That's a good 'un, Goober!" The men grinned and nodded at each other.

"What are you talking about?" I screeched.

"I thought I'd just made that clear," Goober said. "Pet cremation. Jason, the guy who was here? His brother owns a pet store. His clients kept bringing in dead pets. They didn't know what to do with them. Jason looked into it and found a way to take care of the remains. For a reasonable fee, of course. Look. This explains it all."

Goober handed me a folded piece of yellow paper. It was a cheap, copied flyer entitled, "Ha-Pet-Ly Ever After." Being a former copy writer, I groaned when I read it. Below the hideous headline was a list of funerary services and fees, ranging from two bucks for lizard "deposition" to $40 for cremation of dogs under 40 lbs. An asterisk after this last entry invited people to, "Ask about our per-pound savings plan."

"As you can see, members of the genus Rattus – mice, gerbils and the like – only fetch $3.50 a head," Goober explained with the calm demeanor of someone reading a fast-food restaurant menu. "So I save them up until I've got enough to make it worth the charcoal. In captivity, rodents can have exceptionally short lifespans. You'd be surprised. It doesn't take long to get a grill full."

My skin crawled like a bucket of fishing worms. "This is...*disgusting!* It's got to be illegal somehow!"

"It's better than burying Fido in the backyard," Goober argued. "Dead bodies carry disease. As the brochure says, people need an effective alternative. Someone's got to do this important work, Val."

"It pays cash money, too," Winky chimed in brightly.

"The start-up costs were minimal," Goober added. "Jason bought us the Weber out back. We pay him twenty bucks every week and a percentage of the profits. When you deduct the cost of charcoal and lighter fluid, and in a good week we can bring in $400."

"You're kidding," I said, suddenly desperate to wash my hands.

"Nope, he's not," Jorge said. "There's plenty of work, too. You interested?"

"Not on your life! That guy. Jason. He delivers the...bodies?"

Goober nodded. "Yeah. In the garbage bags."

I looked over at the bag by the front door. "So, that's what's in the bag he gave you?"

"Affirmative." Goober walked over, picked up the bag and glanced inside. "Looks like about fifty bucks worth. Wanna see?"

"No!" I screeched. I caught myself and softened my tone. "I'll take your word for it."

I grabbed my purse and backed down the hallway, past Goober, toward the front door. I smiled sheepishly at the guys. For a split second, that strange, clashing, pride-and-shame feeling raced through my heart again.

"I'll see you guys later," I said, and waved as I felt for the door handle behind me.

Goober, Jorge and Winky waved back, a blend of confusion and amusement on their faces. I found the knob, yanked the door open and escaped. As I drove away, my mind swirled in a confusing cloud of conflicted feelings. But there *was one* thing I knew for sure.

I would never be able to enjoy the smell of a backyard barbeque again.

Chapter Ten

A SOUND LIKE GUNFIRE made me spew the last sip of my morning cappuccino all over the kitchen sink. I set my cup down and scrambled to the front window. A peek through the blinds at the culprit calmed my thumping heart. It was Jorge's rusty, old Buick.

I watched as Jorge steered the twenty-foot long, gunmetal-grey battle cruiser into my driveway. He cut the ignition. The Buick backfired again. The doors flew open and three guys piled out like Mafia hitmen – but instead of machine guns and suits they had Santa hats and bright-green vests.

Jorge and Goober headed toward Laverne's house. Winky, however, waddled toward my front door. I opened it before the misfit elf had a chance to ring the bell.

"Morning," I said. "What's up?"

"Mornin', Val. Mind if we park here? The Dodge is deader'n a doornail in Laverne's driveway. Don't want to block her in with the Buick, too. I'm hopin' to get the van up and running today."

"Sure. No problem."

Winky looked past my shoulder into my house.

"You need something else?" I asked.

"Yeah. Can I use your crapper? Laverne kept bringin' us stuff to 'taste-test' yesterday. I didn't want to hurt the old lady's feelings or nothing, so I ate what she give me. But Val, I think she darn-near poisoned me. I went home with a belly ache and woke up this mornin' with a butt ready to squirt like a firehose."

I curled my upper lip. "That's not good."

"Shore ain't. But it could just be me. Winnie's always tellin' me I'm lack toast and tolerance."

I opened my mouth to say something, then shut it again. I sighed and let him in.

"THE GUYS STARTED A holiday-light hanging business," I said to Milly as she walked in the door at Griffith & Maas. By some miracle, I'd managed to get to work before her on that Tuesday morning. I felt pretty pleased about it and shot my boss a smug smile.

"Is that so?" she said, barely glancing at me as she passed by my desk.

My smile evaporated. "Yeah. Hold up, Milly. I've got mail for you."

Milly ambled absently back to my desk. "They call themselves the Three X-migos," I said, and handed her a handful of envelopes.

Milly sifted through the letters without seeing at them, then looked at a spot above my head and muttered, "Well, the Three Wise Men was certainly out of the question." She gave a hint of a smile, then turned and shuffled toward the hallway.

"You know, I've been watching them decorate Laverne's place," I called after her. "I have to admit, it looks pretty impressive so far. I told them they could do mine next."

Milly stopped in her tracks and turned around. "I thought you didn't like decorating for the holidays."

I shrugged. "I don't. But I wanted to encourage them. It's better than them incinerating people's pets in the backyard."

"Uh huh," Milly replied. She turned again to head down the hall to her office. I got up and followed her.

"Didn't you hear me, Milly? The guys are barbequing dogs and cats on their grill! I saw a rat in their freezer!"

Milly studied the envelopes and shuffled toward her office door. "That's nice."

Nice? What the? My crinkled brow went slack. *Oh my word! Milly has a secret!*

My friend Milly Halbert never was much of a multi-tasker. So whenever she was weighed down with the task of keeping a secret, she became incapable of doing anything else. Fortunately for me, the only thing easier than spotting when Milly had a secret was getting her to spill the beans. I followed her into her office and closed the door behind me.

"All right, Millicent. What's up?"

Milly's eyes widened at first, then went all googly. She flopped into her office chair. "Oh, Val! I'm dying to tell somebody. I heard Vance talking on the phone last night. I didn't mean to eavesdrop, but...it just happened, you know?"

"What? What did you hear?"

"He was talking with someone about *my ring size!*"

"Geeze, Milly! You've only been going out what – six months? And he already wants to marry you!"

"Wha...?" Milly's mouth flopped open. The letters fell from her hand. "Oh my word, Val. I wasn't thinking *engagement* ring. I was simply thinking *jewelry.* You don't think...no! He isn't actually going to *propose* to me....*is he?*"

A knot the size of a plum formed in the base of my throat. "I couldn't say, Milly. I just couldn't say."

I'D HAD ALL AFTERNOON to digest the news, but the thought of Milly marrying Vance was still causing me heartburn. If she *did* tie the knot, Vance Pantski would become her new best friend. Where would that leave me? Would I be reduced to the status of her lousy employee?

No! Stop being so selfish! I scolded myself. *That isn't fair to Milly. I should be thinking about her happiness. Not worrying about my own.* I pictured Milly and Vance saying their vows. Acid rose in my throat. I took a Tums and forced myself to smile every time she walked by. I told myself I could adjust. It would just take time.

After work, I stopped at the little Publix grocery store in St. Pete Beach. I was out of Tums. And Ty D Bol. When I'd gotten home last night from discovering the guys' rat-infested freezer, I'd succumbed to an OCD scrubbing frenzy that would have made Mr. Clean hang his head in slacker shame. I was also out of food in general, and I needed a dessert for Laverne's party. I was mulling over the idea of making another fruitcake, too. There were only three days left to marinate it in rum. I figured if I baked it tonight, by Friday evening I could have it up to about fifty-proof....

I was in the baking aisle studying the ingredients on a container of plastic-looking candied fruit when a familiar voice sounded behind me.

"So *you're* the one who's responsible for keeping fruitcakes from going extinct."

I turned around. Cold Cuts, my friend and a master of disguise, stood there looking like...well...her cute, auburn-haired self for a change.

"Hey, you! I hardly recognized you without a costume."

Cold Cuts laughed. "You're looking good, Val."

"You, too! Hey, I was going to call you tonight. Laverne's having a dinner party Friday night. You're invited. Can you make it? I told her I wasn't sure. You have a gig in Tallahassee, right?"

"Not until Saturday," Cold Cuts said. "Shooting a senator at 3 p.m."

I glanced around and made a squirrel face. "I wouldn't say that too loudly."

"Ha ha. The holidays and are good money for me, Val. Seems like every politician in the state needs a holiday GIF to send out to their constituents."

"That sounds like interesting work."

Cold Cuts shrugged. "Not really. I make sure they dress the part and don't come off looking too phony."

"Ugh. I bet *that's* not easy."

Cold Cuts raised an eyebrow and tilted her head. "You can say that again. I'm doing the mayor this evening."

"Like I said before, I wouldn't say that too loudly."

Cold Cuts scrunched her eyebrows for a moment and grinned. "You have a point. How about, 'I'm making a video with the mayor.'"

"Better, but still sounds a little hinky."

She shook her head and laughed. "You're right."

"How about, I have an appointment with the mayor?" I suggested.

Cold Cuts bobbled her head, trying the idea on in her mind. "That works. Anyway, whatever you want to call it, I'm glad for the work. It pays the gas for the old RV." Cold Cuts looked at me as if she were afraid she'd struck a nerve. "Do you still miss it?"

I shrugged. "Not so much. It helps knowing *you* have it."

Cold Cuts smiled. "Thanks for that. So, what's new with *you?*"

"Nothing much. Oh, wait! Milly told me today that she thinks Vance is going to buy her a ring for Christmas. They're moving pretty fast, don't you think?"

Cold Cuts shrugged. "I dunno. They're both grownups. And they've been seeing each other for what – half a year? I'd say that was enough time to know if somebody's looney toons. What about you and Tom? You guys have been going out for a couple of years now, right?"

"No. Eighteen months and nine days. But I'm in no hurry."

"It *sounds* like you are. Counting the *days?*"

"No. I mean, *yes*. I mean, I did count the days. This afternoon. But only after I heard about Milly. It was just a little informal tally. I was curious."

Cold Cuts eyed me with skepticism. "Uh huh."

I frowned. "I'm *serious*. I want to take it slow with Tom. I mean like *glacier* slow. You know, I've never even spent the night at Tom's place."

Cold Cuts smirked. "Sounds like a control issue to me."

I scowled. "Ha ha. Very funny. I hate to admit it, but every time I think about taking the next step with Tom, all I can see is the door to my cage slamming shut."

Cold Cuts' left eyebrow raised and inch. "Really? So, whose hand is doing the slamming?"

I scowled harder. "So, are you going to Laverne's party or not?"

"That depends. Are you bringing a fruitcake with you?"

"Which one?" I sneered.

Cold Cuts laughed, then her eyes grew wide. "Val! Speaking of fruitcakes, did you see the woman in the liquor aisle?"

"What? No...."

"Oh, man! She's too good to miss. Come on!"

Cold Cuts dragged me by the arm toward the back of the store. We scuttled along, heads down, to a four-foot tall bunker of canned green beans, where we hunched like soldiers expecting enemy fire. She peeked cautiously around the right side of the pyramid of cans. "Cool. She's still there. Take a look!"

Cold Cuts relinquished her position. As I scooted to the edge to take a look, she rambled on about the strange woman. "Can you believe it?" she squealed. "Bleach-blonde bouffant. Trailer-trash shirt..."

One peek and I recognized her instantly.

"...red cowboy boots! Ha ha! Have you ever seen such an absolute hayseed in all your life? And the unicorn keychain? Classic!"

"Shhh! I know that hick! She's my cous –" I lost my footing and fell, shoulder-first, into the stack of canned beans. They collapsed in on us like dominoes, then scattered and rolled every which way across the concrete floor like a herd of escaped mice.

"Ugh! Get off me." Cold Cuts grunted. I'd landed face-to-face on top of her.

Tangled together, we wrestled to get up as hollow, clomping footsteps drew ever closer. From the corner of my eye, I saw a flash of red.

"You gal's all right?" Tammy asked. Her face registered surprise, then shock, then something I couldn't define. "Why Cousin Val. I didn't know you played it both ways. Wait 'til your momma finds out."

"What?" I looked down and realized my hand had come to rest on Cold Cut's right breast. I yanked it away, rolled off Cold Cuts and sat on the floor. "It's not what you think –"

I glanced over at Cold Cuts. She laughed, scooted over and kissed me on the cheek. "Are you all right, sweetheart?" she said in a deep baritone.

Tammy's eyes lit up. I could almost hear her dialing my mother's number. Her lips curled into an evil grin. "Well, I'll be."

My face grew hot. I lurched to my feet and forced some words from my mouth. "I'm glad to see you're all right, Tammy. You disappeared on me."

Tammy rolled her eyes. "Give me a break. I came on vacation to have a *good time*, Val. Not go to bed at nine o'clock like an old fart."

Cold Cuts cocked her head at me. "You go to bed at nine o'clock?"

I scowled. "Not *always*."

"What's with all the booze?" Cold Cuts asked Tammy. My redneck cousin was lugging a plastic basket full of bottles of spiced rum. "Big party tonight?"

"They don't carry this kind in Greenville," she replied, then shot me another evil grin. "I kind 'a like it."

A tall, big-boned man walked up beside Tammy and looked at her expectantly. The guy was huge – over six feet and well over 200 lbs. He wore a dress shirt, jeans, and an expensive-looking pair of cowboy boots with silver plated, pointed toes. But the man's most outstanding feature was his nose. It was a spot-on double for a flaccid penis. Once I saw it, I couldn't take my eyes off it.

"This is Richard," Tammy said. She lifted her chin and sniffed.

Richard extended a giant hand toward me. I reached out to shake it, but even though his hand was as big as an oven mitt, I missed it midair. My eyes were fixed like Crazy Glue on his pornographic nose. When he spoke, his obscene proboscis wobbled up and down in a rude, yet hypnotic fashion.

"Hello, there. My friends call me Rich."

"Nice to meet you, Dick." I heard my misspoken words echo in the air as the blood drained from my face. I scrambled to erase my error. "I mean, Ditch." My mouth was suddenly as dry as the Sahara. "I mean, Dick." Paralysis overtook my brain.

"Hi, I'm Cold Cuts," a voice reverberated beside me, as if from underwater. "Nice to meet you Tammy. And Rich."

Tammy gave me the stink eye. "Yeah. You, too."

"As you can see, my girlfriend isn't feeling too well," Cold Cuts said. She wrapped an arm around my waist. "We've got to be going. Enjoy your holidays!"

Before anyone could say another word, Cold Cuts tugged me toward the women's restroom. She remained silent as a stone until she'd managed to shove me through the washroom door. Then she shook her head and burst out laughing.

"Was it just me?" I asked, still too horrified to even stand up straight.

"Are you kidding? I've *never* seen a fake dick that looked as much like a real dick as that guy's nose-dick did!"

"I'm so embarrassed." I shook my head, still in shock. "How are we going to get out of here?"

Cold Cuts cracked open the bathroom door and peeked outside. "We'll make a run for it...as soon as the cock is clear."

Good thing we were in a restroom, or I'd have peed my pants.

WE HOLED UP IN THE john at Publix until Tammy, her large friend and their basket of booze went through the checkout line and out the door. Cold Cuts and I parted ways, with a promise to meet again at Laverne's. I bought my groceries and candied fruit, and was unpacking them at home when I realized I'd forgotten the Ty D Bol. I guess, given the circumstances, two out of three wasn't bad.

Two fruitcakes were baking away in the oven when the doorbell rang. It was Greasy, the freckled-face elf.

"Hi Winky. What's up?"

"Still can't get the van to start, gaul-dang it." He scratched his buzz-cut with the end of an oily wrench. "I think it's the transmission. Anyways, wanted to let you know we're near-bout done at Laverne's. We can start at yore place tomorrow."

"Oh. Okay."

"Got any lights?"

"Huh?"

Winky raised a pale, ginger eyebrow. "Christmas lights?"

"Oh. Yeah, I think so. In the garage. Remember all those ones we found when we cleaned out this place?"

"Lord, help," Winky said, and shook his head. "Them thangs is prob'ly more tangled up than a skunk ape's nostril hair."

I shrugged. "Well, they're all I got." I looked out the door, past Winky and across the road. Goober was hanging a yellow flyer on my neighbor's front doorknob. My heart skipped a beat. I trotted past Winky into the front yard. All along the street, yellow papers attached to mailboxes and front doors fluttered in the breeze like harbingers of impending disaster.

"What is he *doing?*" I asked, even though I already knew.

"Advertisin'," Winky said. He rubbed his belly underneath his green vest. "Now show me them lights."

I heaved a big sigh and walked back inside to open the garage. When I went outside again to show Winky the boxes, Cold Cuts drove up in Glad's old RV.

"Well hey there, young lady!" Winky hollered over to her.

She waved out the window. "Hey back at you!"

"What you doing up in these here parts?"

"Just shot a video with...," Cold Cuts eyed me and grinned, "uh...*for* the mayor."

"Ain't you a big shot!"

Cold Cuts laughed. "Nah. Did you know he lives right up the street?"

"Shore didn't."

"So what are you up to, Winky?"

"We got us a gig hangin' Christmas lights. Just done Laverne's place. Fixin' to start on Val's tomorrow."

"Oh! You ought to totally go check with the mayor. That guy's so busy, he hasn't even put up a tree yet."

"That sounds like an excellent idea," Goober said as he walked up the drive toting a stack of cheap yellow brochures. "Here, take a couple of these, Cold Cuts. Let me know if anyone you know might be in need of our services."

"Sure! Lots of people don't like to do their own –" Cold Cuts glanced at the flyer, then back at Goober. "Pet cremation?"

"Roger that."

I winced when Cold Cuts raised an eyebrow and shook her head. But my mouth fell open when she grinned and said, "Oh my word! That's bloody brilliant!"

Chapter Eleven

WEDNESDAY WENT BY UNEVENTFULLY, as far as my life typically went. I got dressed, gave three derelict elves free reign of my house, bought a bottle of rum, and went to work.

When I got home, things weren't quite as I'd left them.

For one thing, the guys had dragged out the entire contents of my garage and strewn it all over the place. A random passerby couldn't be faulted for thinking a yard sale had recently detonated on my lawn. As I drove up, Jorge was standing in the middle of the junk heap, busily doodling in a notepad. Winky and Goober were rummaging through dilapidated cardboard boxes and playing tug-of-war with knotted strings of old holiday lights.

Yesterday, Jorge had asked me if I'd had any ideas for a lighting design. I'd told him to surprise me. But today, it was Goober who delivered the biggest surprise. When I went to fetch some cold drinks for the guys, I discovered a large, black garbage bag inside my fridge. My gut dropped four inches and I nearly gagged.

I slammed the fridge door and ran outside. I found Goober pilfering through an old box of Christmas decorations. Somehow, he'd managed to get glitter all over his moustache.

"Come with me, Goober," I demanded.

"Aren't you going to read me my rights?"

"You won't need them. I might kill you, instead."

Goober's jovial face went blank. "Oh."

I hustled him into the house and up to the fridge. "What's in the bag, Goober?"

"Of which bag are you speaking?"

"The one in the refrigerator!" I looked around and added, "And any others you might have stashed around here!"

Goober smoothed his bushy, glittery moustache with his thumb and index finger as he contemplated my demands. "Client privilege restricts my ability to answer some more invasive questions."

If he hadn't looked so ridiculous in his Santa hat and glitter moustache, I'd have knocked him one on his peanut-shaped skull. "Goober!"

Goober cocked his head and let out a long, slow sigh. "All right." He straightened his back and tugged on the collar of his green vest. "Remember that bulldog we borrowed from Laverne's neighbor? During my royal pet-strollering days?"

"You mean Buster?"

"That's the one."

My mind took a millisecond to add two and two together. The sum made my stomach turn. "No! That's *Buster?* In the...? No!"

Goober shot me a smug smile. "And you said advertising wouldn't pay off."

"No, no, no!" My lunch knocked on the backdoor of my throat. "Goober! Get it out of my fridge! *Now!*"

"Geeze. I was just trying to keep him fresh before the funeral, so to speak."

"*Now!*"

"All right, already. It's not like you had anything in there, anyway." Goober opened the fridge and yanked the garbage bag out from between the two empty bottom shelves. He slung the bag over his shoulder. When it hit his back with a whump, it almost knocked him breathless. I showed no mercy.

"Out!"

Goober wheezed and stumbled toward the front door. I pushed it open with my foot and stood aside to let him pass.

"No more animals in the house, *dead or alive*. Got it?"

Goober smirked. "Affirmative."

I was closing the door when Winky came waddling up. "We're gonna be working late tonight," he said. He lifted his Santa hat, scratched a spot on his ginger buzz cut, then gave me a proud grin. "Yep. We got to get to the mayor's place after this."

Winky grinned at me like a demented gnome.

My mouth fell open. "What? You guys got the job?"

"Woo hoo! Yessiree! Old Cold Cuts put in a good word for us. I guess that means we're official government men, now."

TRUE TO HIS WORD, WINKY and his two-elf crew worked until sunset. It was a strange and oddly mesmerizing sight. So much so that a couple of people stopped their cars and took pictures of the light-stringing trio of Santa's helpers. Around dinnertime, I was outside admiring the spectacle myself when Laverne walked over, carrying a big tray wrapped in tin foil. Goober and Jorge were on the roof. Winky, who had been standing beside me, took off running behind the house.

"Hi, Laverne," I said.

"Hi, honey! It's looking good around here. Can't wait 'til Friday when they hit the light switch!"

I laughed. "Me either. What you got there?"

"Something I've been cooking up. Could you give it a taste test for me?"

"Sure."

Laverne folded back the foil to reveal something that looked a bit like a pan of deep fried cornbread, but was a strange, burnt-orange color. It was cut into squares like brownies. I took the smallest piece and broke the corner off it. I popped it in my mouth as Laverne watched me intensely, her mouth opening and closing as her horsey jaw chewed along with me.

The stuff was bland and greasy, with a stringy, spongy texture that forced me to stifle my gag reflex.

"What is it?" I asked.

Laverne smiled tentatively. "Sweet potato soufflé."

"Oh." I tried to swallow. It didn't go willingly.

"How was it?" Laverne asked with puppy-dog eyes.

"Interesting. Did you take the skins off?"

"Off what?"

"The sweet potatoes."

Laverne frowned. "They have skin?"

"Yes."

Laverne grimaced in horror and stared into the dish, her eyes as big as poached eggs. "Oh my gosh, Val! I thought they were *vegetables!*"

My jaw went slack. Laverne had left me speechless, yet again. I studied her face as it changed from shock to a determined scowl. Finally, she nodded her head with determination.

"Thanks, honey." Lavern turned and walked back toward her place, toting the foil-covered abomination.

The second Laverne's front door shut behind her, Winky peeked around the corner. "That wasn't the orange stuff, was it?"

I frowned and nodded.

"You didn't swallow any of it, did you?"

I nodded again.

Winky shook his head. "Uh oh."

My eyebrows met in the middle. "What?"

"Just wait. You'll see."

"Oh my lord, Winky! Is *all* her food that bad?"

"No." He grimaced. "I swear, that was the best one."

"Holy crap! What are we going to do?"

"Yeah? What are we gonna do?" Jorge said as he climbed down the ladder. "We can't stay up on the roof forever."

"I've got an idea," I said. "Jorge, you're a great cook. Could you bring a side dish to the party on Friday?"

"Sure, no problem."

"Good. I will, too. I'll ask everyone else as well. I'll give Laverne a call and let her know that all she needs to do is bake the turkey. I think I can keep an eye on that so she doesn't turn it into a disaster."

"Why call? Why don't you go over and tell her?" Goober called from the roof.

"And risk having to sample something else?" I called back.

"Oh. Point taken."

Winky shook his head. "Whew! Thanks, Val. I thought my only hope was to leave town. But I couldn't rightly do it, 'cause the van's busted down right in her driveway!"

"Don't worry, guys. I've got this. Now don't you think it's time you called it a night?"

"Jes. But Winky's a slave driver."

"Am not!" Winky pouted. "Just wanna be ready for the mayor's all."

"Well, you guys have your job, and I've got mine," I said, and went inside to make the call.

"Hey Laverne?"

"Hi, honey."

On the other end of the phone line, I heard something crash. "Are you okay, Laverne?"

"Oh, fiddlesticks. I dropped my casserole dish."

What a shame. "You know, Laverne, I was thinking. Cooking a big holiday meal is a lot of work for one person. And it's traditional, you know, that everybody brings a covered dish."

"Honey, what would I do with a pile of dishes? I already got more than I need."

"Huh? No, I mean *side* dishes, Laverne. Green beans. Potatoes. Stuff like that. Why don't you do the turkey and let the rest of us all help out by bringing our favorite side dishes?"

"Well, I don't know...."

"It's all settled then! I'll let everybody know. We're all so excited! I'll come over early Friday and help you with the last-minute stuff. How's that?"

"Val, you're sweet as sugar. Like the daughter I never had."

That pesky lump resurfaced in my throat. "Thanks, Laverne."

I hung up and wiped a tear from my eye. *Geeze, I'm going soft in my old age.* Maybe it was all that talk of love and marriage.... I shook my head to clear it, then went outside to tell the guys.

"Okay. It's done. I called her," I said as the Three X-migos wrapped it up for the night.

Winky patted me on the back. "You're a bona fide Christmas miracle-worker, Val."

I smirked. "Thanks. But it ain't over 'til it's over."

Chapter Twelve

SOMETHING SCRAMBLING across my roof woke me from a fitful sleep. I tried to get up, but my arms and legs were as heavy as wet cement. My belly gurgled. *Ugh!* One bite of Laverne's caustic casserole had done me in. I'd spent the night running back and forth to the toilet, barely able to catch a wink between bouts of nausea and diarrhea. Whatever had been in that casserole wanted out of my body, and badly.

I opened an eye and blinked up at the ceiling, too exhausted to care about what kind of creature was shuffling around on the shingles overhead. I dragged myself out of bed and stumbled into the kitchen. I hoped a cappuccino might ignite a spark of life in me. It did. But just as the coffee began to work its caffeine magic, a thought snuffed out the fledgling flame.

Tom's precinct party was tonight. *Crap on a cracker.*

I needed to get ready for work, but I had other priorities. In a numb haze, I fumbled around in the fridge for the fruitcakes. At this late stage, I couldn't afford to miss a single marinating session.

When I peeled back the plastic shroud on one, the alcohol vapors stung my dog-tired eyes. As I doused the cake with rum, it took all my remaining willpower to avoid sloshing some, for medicinal purposes, into my cappuccino. I won that round.

I shoved the sodden cakes back into the fridge and padded to the bedroom. Weary to the bone, I tugged a work blouse and skirt onto my zombie body, dragged a brush through my hair and stumbled out the front door. When I turned the ignition on Maggie, the sound of her V-8 engine brought Winky and Jorge running from the side yard.

"Mornin' Val Pal!" Winky called.

"Morning," I groaned. I looked up and noticed my roof was covered with a blue tarp.

"Ha ha! No peeking!" Jorge said, way too cheerily. "You said you wanted it to be a surprise."

I gave the guys the best smile I could muster, given the circumstances.

"See yore sufferin' from the casserole craps," Winky said, shaking his head. "It'll pass." Winky caught his unintentional pun and laughed. "It'll pass, all right, whether you want it to or not!"

"How long?" I asked. My question had been about my recovery period. Winky took it for something else.

"He puffed out his green-vested chest. "Like I tole you yesterday, we got to wrap it up today. We're expected at the mayor's house ASAP."

I let out a bone-tired sigh. "Good. Hey...where's Goober?"

Winky motioned with his freckled head toward the roof. "Up there somewheres, hanging from the raptors."

I DRAGGED MYSELF INTO Griffith & Maas fifteen minutes late. Milly gave me some side eye and glanced at the clock on the wall.

"I was about to file a missing persons' report," she said, only half joking.

"Sorry."

"You've been doing so well lately, Val. But today..." She gave me the once-over and stopped mid-sentence. "Whoa! You look like crap! What happened?"

I plopped my purse on my desk and flopped into my chair. "My colon had a duel with Laverne's sweet potato soufflé. Guess who lost."

Milly crinkled her nose. "Oh, crap."

"Exactly. That reminds me, Milly. Could you bring a covered dish to Laverne's dinner tomorrow? The less of her cooking we have to eat, the better our chances of survival."

Milly's eyebrows flew up and inch, then settled back into place. "Sure. No problem." She turned toward her office, then stopped. "Did you ever get ahold of Cold Cuts?"

"Oh. Yeah. I forgot to tell you. I ran into her at Publix – and my cousin, too." I rested my tired head in my hand. "It was weird. Seeing Tammy, I mean. I felt guilty somehow. When she left, I didn't even call my mother to let her know she was gone."

Milly shrugged. "Well, it's not like your mom called *you* and let you know Tammy was *coming*, either."

I sighed. "True. I guess we're even." I slumped in my chair. "Milly, to tell the truth, I just didn't feel like calling Lucille. I'll have to deal with her soon enough."

Milly smirked. "There ought to be a law against having to call Lucille. So, how *is* she...Tammy, I mean?"

"Tammy is Tammy. You know, any other person might have been embarrassed, up and running off like that. But I guess she's like my mom. Remorse isn't in her arsenal of feelings."

Milly nodded in sympathy. "I get that. So what's she doing? Staying at the beach?"

"Oh. She found a guy."

Milly rolled her eyes. "'Natch. What was *he* like?"

"Well, at first glance, he appeared to be a real dickhead."

"Whoa! That's not very nice, even for you, Val!"

"No. I'm serious. I have pictures to prove it."

AT NOON, MILLY MARCHED up to my desk.

"I've made an executive decision, Val. We're the only ones here, and I'm taking the day off tomorrow. What say we close shop *now*...for the holidays. You okay with that?"

I dropped the files in my hands. "Are you kidding? Best Christmas present ever!" I shot Milly a weary, sideways grin. "I thought we weren't exchanging gifts this year."

Milly laughed. "How about you buy me lunch and we'll call it even."

Relief washed over my tired bones. "Works for me. Ming Ming's okay?"

"Perfect."

Ten minutes later, we were sitting at a tiny table for two by the front window of the small, strip-center restaurant. After we ordered our food, Milly began giggling. She leaned over the table and whispered to me.

"Let me see that picture again."

I laughed and scrolled to the photo Cold Cuts had surreptitiously taken of Tammy and Rich as they'd stood together in the checkout line at Publix. I handed Milly my cellphone. She shook her head in disbelief.

"It's truly uncanny, Val. His nose *does* look exactly like a penis!"

"I know. Poor guy. And now Tammy's his girlfriend. Some people have all the rotten luck."

Milly laughed. "Looks are such a tricky thing. I once broke up with a guy because he had a big gap between his two front teeth. Does that make me petty?"

I shrugged. "Maybe. But it's still better than dropping all your standards just to get laid."

Milly started to reply, but looked up to the left and blushed. I followed her eyes. The waiter was standing there with our sushi rolls, trying his best to stifle a smirk. Milly and I cringed. The waiter cleared his throat and put the plates in front of us. When I looked back at Milly, her face was crimson. From the heat emanating from my cheeks, I was pretty sure mine was, too.

I picked up my chopsticks and toyed with my food. "Subject change. Any more news on the ring?"

"No," Milly managed with a mouthful of sushi.

"Huh. So, what are you getting Vance for Christmas?"

Milly's eyes lit up. "A weekend getaway at the beach!"

I nodded, impressed. "Nice."

Milly spoke in a soft, dreamy tone. "Vance works so hard at his restaurant. I've already worked it out with his sister and the bar staff so he can be gone two nights. I'm so excited to be able to surprise him! How about you? What are you getting Tom?"

I bit my lip and blew out a breath. "I dunno."

Milly's voice went screechy. "What? You haven't got his present yet? Val! How *could* you?"

"You know I hate to shop, Milly. And I haven't been in a holiday mood, what with this trip to my mom's coming up."

"Val, you can't let your mother ruin your life from 400 miles away."

I scowled. "I'm not!"

Milly arched an eyebrow almost to her hairline.

I winced. "Crap! You're right. How does she *do* it, Milly?"

Milly shook her head. "*She* doesn't, Val. *You* do it to *yourself.*"

I frowned and looked down at my plate. "Part of me *gets* that, Milly. But the other part of me feels like I'm...I dunno...*doomed.*" I looked up at Milly again. "Ever since I saw that tree in the park, I feel like I've been lassoed by some horrible tractor beam. It's pulling me toward a show-down I have *no hope* of winning. *You've* met them, Milly. The women in my family are so...so...*competitive.*"

Milly curled her upper lip. "That's putting it mildly."

I dropped my chopsticks onto my plate and slumped back in my chair. "They'll hand you a glass of sweet tea with one hand and stab you in the back with the other. They're...they're...."

"Crazy."

"Yes! Milly, I'm so worried. What will Tom think?"

Milly laughed. "Val, it's not like you have the only pile of weird relatives in the world. Tom will understand."

"Thanks."

Milly winked. "And if he doesn't, you can always steal old dick-face away from Tammy."

I laughed despite myself. "Millicent Halbert. Always there with a kind word of encouragement."

Milly grinned. "I do my best."

Chapter Thirteen

WHEN I GOT HOME FROM lunch with Milly, I changed into a t-shirt and shorts and popped over to see Laverne. I needed to make sure her main course tomorrow wasn't going to be ptomaine turkey. I rang the doorbell. Laverne, who was always perfectly coiffed and made-up, came to the door looking as if she'd just completed a thirty-mile marathon through the Amazon.

"Geeze! Are you okay, Laverne?"

Laverne wiped her sweaty forehead with a kitchen towel. "Thank goodness you're here, honey! I need help with the turkey. I can't lift it."

"Oh. Okay. I can do that."

Laverne's worried face brightened a notch. "I don't remember it being so heavy when I bought it," she said as I followed her down the hall. "I got it to the kitchen, but I can't get it up in the sink to let it thaw."

As we entered the kitchen, my eyes bulged at a black garbage bag on the floor beside the sink. My heart skipped a beat. *Oh no! It couldn't be...*

"I'll take care of it," I said, eyeing the bag with dread.

"Oh, thank you!" Laverne said. She smiled with relief. "I'm warning you, it's a beast!"

I certainly hope not. But I needed to find out for sure. Laverne, however, did not. I needed to create a diversion.

"Laverne, I've got Tom's party to go to tonight. Could I ask a favor? I need to borrow some hairspray."

"Sure!" Laverne beamed a horsey smile my way. "I'll go get it, honey. If you want, I can fix your hair, too, like I did last time."

"Thanks. That'd be great."

Laverne disappeared down the hallway. I closed my eyes, held my breath and patted down the outside of the garbage bag. I felt a paw and retched.

Arrggh!

I opened my eyes, steeled myself, and tried to hoist the bag. It barely cleared the floor. It had to have weighed over forty pounds. Laverne came back in the kitchen holding up a silver spray can. "You want iron hold or platinum shine?"

"Which one is that?"

"Platinum shine."

"I'll take the other one."

"Coming right up!"

Laverne turned back toward the hallway. I snatched the bag by the tie handles and drug it as fast as I could toward the garage door. As I shoved it over the threshold with my foot, the bag tumbled down the step the way a dead body does in the movies. A creepy feeling squirmed along my spine. I shuddered as I dragged the bag across the garage floor to the freezer chest.

I braced myself, opened the freezer door, and took a sideways peek inside. Half covered by a considerable collection of blue-and-white Skinny Dipper cartons, I made out the shape of a frozen turkey in a dark-grey grocery bag. I pulled it out and set it on Laverne's washing machine. Then I squatted, took hold of the garbage bag with both hands, grunted, and heaved the carcass up the side of the freezer and in. I slammed the lid just as Laverne appeared at the garage door.

"What 'cha doing, honey?"

"Huh? Oh. I...I uh...that big old turkey would have never thawed in time, Laverne. I got a smaller one." I picked up the turkey from the washing machine. "See?"

Laverne beamed a horsey smile at me. "Oh, Val. You're always coming to my rescue. Thank you!"

"You're welcome. Happy to do it."

I carried the frozen turkey to the kitchen, relieved we wouldn't be eating Buster for dinner tomorrow night. I was also thankful I wouldn't have to explain where the smaller, "second" turkey had come from. Laverne's faulty-wired brain would never make the connection. But that wasn't giving Laverne enough credit. Unlike my mother, sweet Laverne had no head for devious plots or schemes.

I dropped the turkey in the metal sink with a thud. "There you go, Laverne. And I wanted you to know, I'm off work tomorrow. I should be home all day. If you need help with anything, just holler."

Laverne smiled and held a spray can toward me at arm's length. "Thanks, honey. Here's your spray."

"Huh? Oh! Yes, thanks!" I took the can and turned to leave. Laverne grabbed my arm.

"Honey, I don't know how to mention this, but you might want to change your clothes."

"What? Why?"

"I think you had a little 'accident.'"

I looked down and almost fainted with embarrassment. Heaving Buster into the freezer had proven too much for my compromised colon. I'd seriously crapped my pants.

I TRIED TO TAKE A LONG, hot shower, but my mind wouldn't let me. It plagued me with the irresistible itch to make an urgent call. I dried off, wrapped a towel around my head and dialed Goober. He answered in a polite, business tone.

"Three X-migos. We make sure your holidays are well hung."

"Goober! You need to get your butt over to Laverne's, *right now!*"

"Val? What's flown up your skirt?"

"Are you kidding me? You need to get that dog out of her freezer *immediately!*"

"Huh. How'd you find out?"

"She...*what does it matter?* We almost had roasted bulldog on tomorrow night's menu, okay?"

"Well, given the quality of the offerings so far...."

"*Goober!*"

"All right, already. I'll take care of it on the way back from the mayor's place tonight."

I clicked off the phone and went to collect my crappy clothes from the bathroom floor. I threw them in the washing machine, set it to the industrial clean cycle, and lay down on the couch. Lightheaded from dysentery, lack of sleep and my run-in with Goober, I was in desperate need of a nap.

I'd just nodded off when the doorbell rang. I groaned and hauled my tired, (but clean) butt to the door and peeked out the peep hole. It was Laverne. I cracked open the door.

"Hey. What's up?"

"I'm here to help you get ready for tonight. It's the least I can do. I know you're not feeling too good."

"That's okay. I don't –"

Laverne pushed past me and made her way inside. "Val, when are you gonna learn, honey? You don't have to take on the world alone. You've got friends who want to help."

"But I don't want to put you out, Laverne."

Laverne smiled at me like a mother donkey. "The only way you can put me out is to say 'no' when I offer to help. Don't you realize, sugar? Helping you brings me joy. Don't take that away from me."

Hot tears brimmed my eyes. "All right. I've washed my hair. Do your worst."

I poured us a drink and sat on a kitchen stool while Laverne fussed over my hair and fooled around with my makeup. After what seemed like two hours, she announced she was done.

"Take a look," she said, and handed me a mirror.

She bit her lip in anticipation of my reaction. I braced for *Bride of Frankenstein*, but I got *Here Comes the Bride*. Laverne had worked a miracle on my pallid face and frizzy hair. Even *I* was impressed.

"Wow. Thanks, Laverne!"

Laverne grinned. "My pleasure, honey."

As she zipped up the back of my little black dress, I heard a car pull up in the drive. "That must be Tom."

"I best get going, then." Laverne picked up her hairspray and gave my head one last blast. "That ought to hold you through a hurricane."

I hugged Laverne. "Let's hope it doesn't have to. Now don't forget to take the bag of giblets out of the turkey before you put it in the oven."

"What's a giblet?" she asked.

"The guts. They should be in a paper bag. In the turkey's cavity."

Laverne stared at me, confused. "Turkeys can get cavities?"

If I hadn't been so tired, I'd have laughed out loud. "Tell you what, Laverne. I'll come by tomorrow morning and show you. How's that?"

Laverne sighed with relief. "Whew! That'd be great, sugar." She reached for the doorknob just as Tom rang the bell. She grinned at me, then yanked opened the door and curtseyed. "Good evening, Prince Tom. Let me present to you, your Princess, Val."

A long, low wolf whistle sounded from Tom's lips.

I shook my head and grinned. "And you already know my fairy godmother."

Tom nodded at Laverne. "May I say, ladies, both of you look ravishing."

Laverne laughed. "I look like the dog's dinner."

"Not a chance," Tom said. "And speaking of dinner, I'm looking forward to tomorrow."

Laverne beamed. "Me too. Now you two go have a good time tonight! Fairy godmother's orders!" Laverne hugged me, then Tom, then headed out the door.

Tom closed the door behind her and gave me an admiring once-over. "You look amazing, Val."

"Thanks. You, too."

"You ready?"

"Yes."

As we headed out the front door, Tom grabbed my hand and pulled me close to him. He whispered softly, his lips nearly touching mine. "There's something I want to ask you."

My heart skipped a beat. I wasn't ready for this.... "Oh? Well, I want to ask you something, too."

Tom smiled dreamily. "What's that, sweetheart?"

"Tom, is there a law against cremating animals in your backyard?"

Tom drew back sharply, like a needle scratching over a record. "What? I...I don't know. Why do you ask?"

I shrugged and stepped out the door. "Just curious."

AS TOM AND I STROLLED into the party at the police precinct, heads didn't turn like they did when I'd worn my painted-on, red sequined dress last year. But my little black dress did catch the attention of a few wandering cop eyes. Tom puffed up like a peacock as he led me toward a group of men gathered around the buffet table. He was about to introduce me to some of his buddies when the inevitable happened. We had a run-in with Tom's nemesis, Lt. Hans Jergen.

"Lieutenant Foreman."

"Lieutenant Jergen."

Having exchanged dirty looks and the briefest possible greetings, Jergen turned his attention to me. He looked me up and down in a way that made me want to take a bath in bleach.

"Well, if it isn't Ms. Fremden. Nice to see you again," he said with the charm and sincerity of a door-to-door toilet-brush salesman.

After all the hell Jergen had put Tom through earlier in the year, it was all I could do to remain civil in the public sphere. So I kept my answer short. "You, too."

As I studied Lt. Jergen, I realized he looked different. He had pimped his ride. He wore an expensive tailored suit and Italian loafers. Since I'd seen him last, he'd bleached his teeth and found a much, much better barber. If I hadn't known how ugly he was on the inside, I'd have considered him an eligible bachelor worth mentioning to friends. But, like I said, he was rotten inside.

"I hope you two have a pleasant holiday planned," Jergen said with a brilliant-white, fake smile.

"We do," Tom said, and tugged at my hand.

For the brief time necessary, we'd all managed to find a way to tolerate each other's existence, the way political opponents are forced to do. I was glad to see the détente Jergen and I had reached in June appeared to be holding. I'd kept my mouth shut about his secret business, and he'd kept off Tom's butt. When Jergen said "Good evening," and walked away, relief washed over me like a downy blanket. I was too exhausted for a battle tonight.

Once the inescapable head-on collision was over, the party seemed to resume around us, as if time had stood still around us. A plump, happy-looking guy came up to Tom and me.

"Let's get a photo of you two!" said the cop. I recognized him from Davie's Donuts.

"Officer Muller! Nice to see you!"

"You two look like movie stars," Muller said. "Better than that, you two look *happy* together. Say cheese!"

I felt my face flush with pride as Officer Muller snapped a shot of me standing next to Tom. I handed him my cellphone. "Please, would you mind taking a couple with my phone?"

"Happy to oblige." Muller snapped off a quick succession of photos.

"Thanks Muller," I said.

"I'm starving," Tom said. "Come on, Muller. Let's hit the buffet."

Tom tugged me along to the buffet table. Thanks to Laverne's miracle-weight-loss casserole, I looked great in my dress. But I still had no appetite. I looked over the buffet spread. In the center of the table was a whole, roasted pig. I nudged Tom on the elbow.

"That's rather ironic, don't you think?"

Confusion crossed Tom's handsome face for a second. Then his jaw went slack and he shook his head.

"Well, at least it's not in uniform."

Chapter Fourteen

I LAY IN BED AND STRETCHED my arms and legs like a lazy cat. *Ahhh*.

Compared to yesterday, this morning I felt like a million bucks. Then, like an annoying mosquito, my mind buzzed on and stuck me with a thought. *I'll be at mom's place tomorrow.*

My stomach flopped. I reached over for Tom, my warm security blanket. All I got was a handful of cold, wadded sheet. I hitched myself up on one elbow as he came stumbling in, his blond hair a charming bird's nest tangle.

"Morning, princess," he joked.

"Don't start."

"Feeling better?"

The sight of two cappuccinos in Tom's hands made my stomach rumble. For the first time since ingesting Laverne's sabotage soufflé, I felt hungry. Starved, even. I sat up in bed and reached out for a cup.

"I'm so hungry I could eat a horse."

Tom laughed and handed me a cappuccino. "Go easy. I'm saving my appetite for Laverne's. I'm looking forward to a good, home-cooked meal for a change."

"Well, you won't be getting one at Laverne's. Unless, of course, you really *are* hungry enough to eat an actual horse."

Tom sighed and crawled into bed beside me. "Better horse meat than nothing. That's about all that gets cooked around here."

I frowned. "What are you insinuating? I can cook."

"You keep saying that, but so far, you haven't delivered any proof." Tom took a sip of cappuccino. "For all I know, your 'great culinary skills' are just a figment of your imagination."

I elbowed him and sloshed a foamy blob of cappuccino onto the sheet. "*You've* got two hands, Tom. I don't see *you* cooking anything."

"That's because you won't set foot in my place."

I pouted in an unreasonable fashion. "Why should I, when there's a perfectly good kitchen here? Go ahead, knock yourself out. I could go for a cheese omelet."

Tom stared at me, incredulous. "Are you kidding? You don't have any eggs in that empty fridge of yours."

"Humph," I sneered.

"So, what are you going to bring to Laverne's tonight, anyway?"

"A fruitcake. You?"

"I don't know yet. Got any suggestions?"

I eyed him with mock suspicion. "What can you cook that won't kill us all?"

Tom twisted his lip sideways. "I've been told I make a mean batch of mashed potatoes."

I smiled and closed my eyes as my empty stomach savored the thought. "Mmmm. Mashed potatoes. Sound yummy." I opened my eyes again. "For the record, I like mine lumpy."

"That figures." Tom set his cup on the nightstand and snuggled next to me. He and ran a warm hand under my nightgown and along my grumbling tummy. "You never have been one to like things too smooth and easy."

AS TOM DROVE AWAY, I waved from the front door and breathed a heavy sigh of relief. I'd made it through another morning without the dreaded "Christmas present discussion." I still had no idea what

Tom was getting me, or what I was going to get him. In desperation, I padded over to the computer and googled "gifts for him." I sifted through a couple hundred of the eighty-million search results. I was about to order a crate full of man-bacon when I realized I'd waited too late. Tom and I were shipping out for my mother's place at eight o'clock tomorrow morning. The crate would never arrive at my house on time, and I didn't dare ship it to Greenville. The whole town would be gossiping about it before the mailman set foot on my mother's doorstep.

A nauseating thought struck me. I googled "home pet cremation." To my utter amazement, there were *zero* results. I didn't think that was even possible! I turned off the computer and went to the kitchen to douse more rum on the fruitcakes. At least I had tonight's dessert under control.

Under control...under control.... Oh, crap! I forgot to check in with Laverne this morning!

As I grabbed the knob on my front door, the doorbell rang at precisely the same moment. The unexpected buzz startled me like an electric shock. I yanked open the door. Laverne was standing there looking as if she'd run over my dog. Luckily, I didn't have one.

"I think something's wrong with the turkey," she said, her eyes on the verge of panic.

"What do you mean?"

"I went to check on it but it won't let me."

"Huh?"

Laverne grabbed my hand. "Come on. I'll show you."

I slipped on some flip-flops and followed Laverne's skinny, jean-covered butt to her back door, dread growing with every step. I imagined a blackened turkey carcass smoldering on the counter...a raw turkey caught in the garbage disposal...a bag of giblets boiling away in the paper bag they came in. But nothing could have prepared me for what she'd *actually* done.

Laverne opened the front door and the delicious smell of roasting turkey was overpowering. I followed her into the kitchen and up to the stove. Laverne turned and looked at me with wide, puzzled donkey eyes. "It won't let me in."

"What?"

Laverne tried to open the oven door. It wouldn't budge. "See? The stove says the door's locked. How could the turkey lock the door, Val?"

I took a slow breath to calm myself before I spoke. "Laverne, I think you put the oven on clean."

Laverne nodded her head. "Yes! Yes! I'm sure of it, Val. That oven was clean when I turned it on. I've never even used it before."

I bit my lip. "No. I mean, Laverne, you set the oven's self-cleaning program."

"Self-cleaning program?" Laverne smiled and shook her head with admiration. "Wow! What will they think of next?"

"That's *not* good news, Laverne. We need to stop it."

Laverne's worried donkey face returned. "Oh. So, how do you do that?"

"I dunno. Do you have the manual?"

Laverne pursed her lips, patted her pockets and looked up and to her left. "Manual?"

I blew out a breath. "Never mind. Let's call Winky. He's the mechanical genius in the family."

Laverne smiled at me, a glimmer of hope in her eyes. "That's a great idea."

"I'm going to need to use your phone, Laverne."

"Oh. Sure." Laverne handed me a cellphone. "Hit #23."

I did as instructed, but curiosity got the better of me while I waited for Winky to pick up. "Why #23, Laverne?"

"For W," Laverne said, as if she were explaining the obvious. "It's the 23rd letter of the alphabet."

I heard someone pick up. "Winky?"

"The Three X-Migos. We make sure –"

"Winky! It's me. Val.!"

"Oh. Hey there."

"Listen! We've got a situation here at Laverne's."

"Uh oh. Is the old bird okay?"

"Yes. But the turkey's on lockdown."

Chapter Fifteen

THE SWEATY, FRECKLED, elf-man grunted and groaned as he pulled the oven way from the wall, unplugged it, and removed several strange-looking metallic parts from the back of it. Winky scratched his arm with a screwdriver and made his diagnosis.

"We're gonna have to let her ride."

"What do you mean?" I asked.

Winky looked up from his seated position on the floor next to the stove. "I've done all I can do, Val. We're just gonna have to wait 'til the oven cools down enough for the lockin' mechanism to release on its own."

"Not good."

In the time since Laverne and I had called Winky for help, a dull grey smoke had begun to pour from the center of one of the stove's cooking elements. It had the aroma of charred metal.

"What about all the smoke?" I asked.

Winky shrugged. "Open the winders." Winky grunted and pulled himself to standing. "I figure it's over 800 degrees in that there oven by now. Good thing is, now that it ain't got no current no more, the temperature's got nowheres to go but down."

"Thank you, Winky, hon," Laverne said. She hugged him and went over to open the kitchen window and let in the flies.

Winky tipped his Santa hat. "I'll be at the mayor's if you need me." As he said the word "mayor," he puffed out his chest. "All right if we drop by your place to clean up afterwards, Val? We been workin' our hind-ends off all week. It'd be nice to save the ride all the way back to Jorge's before dinner tonight."

I cringed at the prospect of three dirty elves molesting my bathroom. "Sure. No problem."

"All righty then, I'm off." Winky turned, took a step toward the front door, then turned back around. "Oh, Val? I've been so gaul-darn busy with the Christmas light stuff that I hat'n had no time to fix the van. Winnie and me was plannin' to head up to see my family up near Lake City tomorrow. Any chance we could hitch a ride with you and Tom?"

"I...uh...don't see why not. I'll talk to Tom about it."

"Much obliged." Winky smiled and headed out the front door.

Laverne smiled sweetly. "The way you two take care of each other, you'd think you were brother and sister."

I shook my head and laughed. "Not likely, Laverne. Nobody in *my* family is *that* nice."

Laverne bit her lip, then frowned with guilt. "I'm sorry about the turkey, Val. I should have called you before I put it on to bake."

I shook my head. "No. It's my fault. I should have come over earlier. I know you're doing your best, Laverne. Now, don't worry about it. Everybody's bringing something to eat. It'll all work out."

Laverne's guilty look took on a tinge of hopefulness. "You think so?"

"Sure. I'll be back around six to help you finish up. In the meantime, if the stove bursts into flames or something, call me, okay?"

"Okay," Laverne nodded.

WHEN I GOT BACK TO my place, I checked my phone. There was a text from Winky.

"Plan B, pick up some fried chicken."

I texted back a smiley face and headed for the bathroom. I smelled of smoke and desperation. Not a particularly appealing combination.

I showered and slipped into a paisley patterned sundress with red shoulder straps and three crimson buttons down the front. Even though it was December 20, the days had barely begun to dip into the 70s. I rifled through a drawer and dug out my only sweater in case, by some miracle, it got cool enough to need it. I'd finished blow-drying my hair and brushing on a little makeup when the guys arrived. They looked like three worn-out garden gnomes.

"You guys be gentle with the facilities, okay?" I half-joked, then grabbed one of the fruitcakes out of the fridge and went to help Laverne.

Laverne came to the door in a flowing white gown that stopped at her ankles to show off her gold spike heels. Her dress and hair reminded me of a movie star pinup from the 1940s. But despite her regal appearance, she fretted and pranced around me like a nervous Nelly. I'd never seen her so out of sorts.

"Laverne! What's gotten into you?" I asked.

"I used to hold fancy dinner parties in Vegas for the big wigs," Laverne confessed. "But that was so long ago I can't even remember the difference between a salad fork and a steak knife."

She led me to the table she'd laid out for us. It was stunning. Spode Christmas plates and red-stemmed wine glasses rested neatly on a beautiful red, green and gold plaid tablecloth. Green cloth napkins stood like small Christmas trees in the center of each plate. A pot of miniature poinsettias in a gold container served as the centerpiece, flanked by a pair of silver candelabras.

"Wow. This is fancy, Laverne! Like dinner at the Vanderbilt's!"

Laverne blushed. "It's not *that* fancy."

"Hey, you're using *real plates*. For most of us, that's a special occasion."

Laverne grinned. "At my age, being *alive* is a special occasion."

I laughed and hugged Laverne. "Relax. Everything is beautiful. Including you. You look like a film star in that dress! Now tell me, is there anything else that needs doing?"

Laverne beamed. "Well, I've still got to get the cranberry sauce out of the cans."

"I better do it. I'd hate for you to get a spot on that nice, white dress. Take a tip from me," I winked. "Wear patterned clothes to dinner. Hides the food stains."

The doorbell rang. I raised an eyebrow at Laverne. "Somebody's early. Are you ready, hostess with the mostess?"

Laverne grinned. "I think so." She strolled to the door and opened it with panache. Tom stood in the doorway holding a bottle of wine in one hand, a tub of mashed potatoes in the other. "This is for you, lovely lady," Tom said, and handed off the wine to Laverne. I felt a surge of pride, and smiled at Tom in a way I hoped conveyed it.

"Why, thank you, sweetheart!" Laverne gushed. "Come on in the kitchen with those potatoes. I'll set them on the oven to keep warm." Laverne winked at me as she passed. I felt a warm glow inside me that grew even warmer as Tom brushed a kiss on my cheek.

The doorbell rang again. This time I answered it. Cold Cuts arrived with a bouquet of flowers and a beautiful covered dish. *Crap! All I brought was my ugly little fruitcake.* "You're making me look bad," I said.

"No way, Val. You're gorgeous."

I grinned. "You, too, kiddo."

Cold Cuts smiled smugly. "I know."

We laughed and hugged each other, then went into the kitchen where Laverne was handing Tom a can opener. "You sure you know how to use that thing?" she asked.

Tom grinned. "Ma'am, if I didn't, I'd have starved to death a long time ago."

Laverne cackled with laughter. I heard a knock at the door and went back to find the Three X-migos had arrived, fresh from the showers and, to my disappointment, without their Santa caps. Jorge was holding a huge, rectangular container made of aluminum. The top was covered in foil. "Where should I put this?" he asked.

"Hi, you guys! I'll take that," Laverne said from behind me.

"No ma'am," Jorge said. "It's heavy. I'll follow you to the kitchen." Jorge kissed Laverne on the cheek. She flashed her pearly white dentures and blushed.

"What's in the container?" I asked Winky as Jorge passed by.

He shrugged. "Dunno. Jorge said it was a recipe of his papa's."

"Where's Winny?"

"She had to work. But she'll be here soon."

My phone buzzed. It was a text from Milly. I walked into the kitchen and made the announcement. "Milly says she and Vance are running late and we should start without them."

"Nonsense," Laverne said. "We'll wait a few more minutes. Anyone want a glass of wine?"

"Sure!" our voices mingled into one.

Tom popped the cork on a bottle of wine while Winky entertained us with his one-redneck stand-up routine.

"What do you call an alligator detective?" Winky asked.

"I don't know. What?" Laverne asked.

"An in-vest a gator."

Laverne giggled like a little girl. It was all the encouragement Winky needed to continue.

"What did stuttering Santa say when Rudolf wanted to hire a prostitute?"

"What?" Cold Cuts asked.

"Just say no no no to the ho ho ho."

I groaned, then laughed despite myself. "That was awful, Winky. Don't be giving Tom any ideas. His jokes are bad enough already."

I looked over at Tom. He feigned a hound-dog pout and pulled the cork from a wine bottle with a 'pop.'

"You didn't think that was funny, Val?" Winky asked. He hung his head. "Well, on a sad note, I runned over a deer on the way home last night."

"That's awful!" Laverne said. "Did you kill it?"

"No. I knocked it about twenty feet up in the air. When it come down, its leg was busted, but the red light on his nose was still working fine."

Cold Cuts and I looked at each other and groaned. Winky pointed his finger at us like a gun. "Got'cha!"

Laverne handed out the glasses of wine while Tom poured. She pulled a cold drink out of the fridge for Jorge.

"Everybody have something to toast with?" she asked.

"Yes!" We held up our glasses.

"To family," Laverne said.

A knot clotted my throat. Everyone looked around and smiled merrily at each other and echoed her toast. "To family!"

Before I could clear the knot to speak, Winky beat me to it.

"Let's eat!" he hollered. "I'm hungry as a newborn tapeworm."

Yuck! There went my appetite.

"Everybody grab your side dish and take it to the table," Tom commanded. Like dutiful children, we all assembled around Laverne's beautiful table. Tom took the cover off his dish of mashed potatoes. They looked especially lumpy. I shot him a grin. Cold Cuts grimaced and opened her container. It was full of mashed potatoes, too.

"Dang!" Winky said. "Oh well. At least we got Jorge's papa's stuff."

Jorge peeled away the foil covering his container. "*Lo siento.* It's *purée de pappas.* That's Spanish for mashed potatoes."

Cold Cuts burst out laughing. Her contagious giggle spread like wildfire around the table.

"We've also got cranberry sauce," Tom piped up.

"And fruitcake!" I added.

"Then I suggest we partake, before the potatoes get cold," Goober said.

We all settled into our seats around the table. Winky plopped a heaping spoonful of Cold Cuts' potatoes onto his plate when the doorbell rang.

"Ain't that always the way?" he griped, then grinned.

Before anyone could get up, the front door opened with a squeak. A second later, Vance and Milly appeared, holding a bottle of wine and a covered dish.

"What did you bring?" Winky hollered. "Not smashed taters, I hope."

"No," said Vance.

Everyone sighed with relief.

"I brought my mother's specialty," Vance continued. "New England boiled red-skin potatoes!"

"Gaul-dang it!" Winky hollered.

Everyone around the table burst out laughing. Milly and Vance took a look at the other offerings and shrugged. "Ooops!"

"Please, take a seat," Laverne said.

"Should we say a prayer before we eat?" Jorge asked as Milly and Vance scooted in around the table.

"Yeah." Winky sneered. "And one after!"

CLICK.

The sound echoed from the kitchen. Everyone went silent.

"It's the dad-burned turkey!" Winky cried out.

Winky jumped up and ran into the kitchen like his short, ginger buzz-cut was on fire. We all scrambled to our feet and assembled like a hungry mob around the perimeters of the kitchen. We stared in morbid anticipation as Winky prepared to do battle with the beast in Laverne's oven. For armor, he chose a reindeer-motif dishtowel. He wrapped it around his head like a turban, then slid his hands into two fluffy snowman oven mitts. He positioned himself in front of the stove door like a baseball catcher.

"Stand back ever'body, I'm goin' in!"

Winky snatched open the door. A plume of black smoke enveloped him. We all coughed and waved our hands around. When the smoke cleared, Winky was standing there holding two charred, black lumps in his oven mitts.

Winky laughed. "Hey Goober, looks like Santa left your lumps a coal here by accident."

Goober grimaced. "What in the world are those?"

"Baked potatoes," Laverne confessed sheepishly.

Her admission sparked a round of roaring laughter. As I wiped tears from my eyes, Winky pulled a large, smoking, black heap from the oven. He heaved the pan onto the stove top, then stood at arm's length away from it. He pulled back the first layer of blackened foil as if it might detonate. But it didn't. Instead, the layers of foil had acted like the heat shield on a space shuttle. Inside, the turkey had cooked to perfection, its skin a perfect shade of golden brown. We all cheered.

"It's a Christmas miracle!" Jorge yelled.

"Waah hoo!" Winky cheered.

"Hallelujah," Goober deadpanned.

Later, as we passed around the platter heaped high with carved dark and light meat, we all agreed it was the best darn turkey we'd ever tasted. When it was time to cut the fruitcake, we were stuffed to the gills with good food and good cheer. When I passed around the slices, I handed Jorge a pudding cup instead.

"Sorry, Jorge," I whispered. "But the cake is full of booze."

Jorge smiled. "No problem, Val. I hate fruitcake. But I love choco-late pudding."

Winky shot me a jealous look. "You got any more a them? I ain't too fond a fruitcakes, myself."

"You could always take a self-help class," Goober said sarcastically.

Winky didn't get the joke.

AFTER DESSERT, WINKY tapped on a glass with a knife to get our attention.

"First off, I want to say that this meal, especially the turkey, was lammin' shore good."

Everyone cheered.

"Second, I want to thank Laverne and Val for their support of the Three X-Migos." Winky and Goober and Jorge nodded at us, their faces shining with gratitude.

"And third, I want to invite ever'body outside for the after-dinner, light-time spectacular."

"What's that?" Laverne asked.

"We're gonna plug in your Christmas lights," Jorge said.

Laverne's eyes lit up. She clasped her hands together and yelled, "Oh, goody!"

Like stuffed partridges, we all waddled out in a line and assembled on the lawn in front of Laverne's house.

"Hit it!" Winky instructed.

From inside the garage, Goober and Jorge got busy plugging extension cords into sockets. Laverne's roof lit up like a searchlight.

On the right side of her roof, outlined in a string of lights, the figure of Santa stood next to some kind of contraption. Shifting rows of red and white lights in the outline of an arm made it appear as if Santa was raising and lowering his arm, shifting a lever on the machine. Every time his arm went down, the numbers "777" flashed. The word "Jackpot" illuminated on the left side of the roof, and the outline of three reindeer lit up. Each kicked up a leg and danced a chorus-line cancan.

"Oh my lord," Laverne cried out. "Boys, you've outdone yourself! That's the prettiest thing I've seen this side of Vegas!"

To be honest, it truly was something to behold. We all stood and watched it go through its cycle a dozen more times. Santa always hit the jackpot. The reindeer always danced.

After a few minutes, Winky spoke up, breaking the silence.

"Now for Val's place," he said, and shot me a sly grin.

"This ought to be good," Tom said. He kissed me and locked his arm in mine. We strolled behind Winky as he picked his way across the lawn to the front of my house. I realized the tarp was gone from my roof. But it was too dark to make out anything else. Tom pulled me close as Goober and Winky disappeared into my garage.

"Now!" hollered Winky.

The roof lit up. Patches of colored lights outlined a woman in a bathing suit lounging in a beach chair. Her right arm moved toward a beer can in her left hand. Lines of white lights appeared to shoot from the can she was holding, as if she'd pulled the tab top on it. As the spray of white lights crossed the roof, the lines blinked out. Stars blinked on, and a message illuminated below them. "Glad Tidings to All."

My ears grew hot and I burst into tears. I buried my face in Tom's chest and sobbed. Tom rubbed my back and hugged me to him.

"Are you okay, Val?" I heard Jorge's voice ask at my right side.

"We didn't mean to hurt your feelings," Winky said from the left.

"It's all a bit dramatic, if you ask me," Goober chimed in.

Goober's comment made me laugh through my tears. I turned my head from Tom's chest and faced the men.

"Oh, guys! My feelings aren't *hurt*. Not at all. They're...they're just...*overflowing*."

Chapter Sixteen

WHOEVER WROTE THAT holiday song, *It's the Most Wonderful Time of the Year*, wasn't kin to the Jolly clan. I hadn't felt this much dread since I'd dropped my taxes off to be calculated by Vinny of Vinny's Discount Tax Filing, Bail Bonds and Cat Boarding.

I stuffed a frumpy, blue-flannel nightgown into my suitcase and zipped it closed. I didn't know why, but the thought of looking sexy anywhere within a fifty-mile radius of my mother made my skin crawl. I lugged the suitcase into the living room and perked another cappuccino. The first sip had just touched my tongue when Tom pulled up. Bless his heart. He was wearing a flannel shirt tucked into his pressed blue jeans. My heart smiled at his effort. He wanted to blend in in Hicksville.

"Hi," I smirked as I opened the door. "Welcome, Paul Bunyan."

"You like it? I'm thinking it's good camouflage." Tom stepped past me into the living room.

"What? No kiss?" I complained.

Tom shot me a boyish grin. "No offence, Val, but either you've got a cappuccino moustache or you've gone rabid."

I curled my upper lip and reached to wipe the milk foam from it, but Tom beat me to it. He grabbed me by the shoulders and licked my mouth like an over-friendly dog. I jerked my face away. "Gross, Tom!"

"What?" Tom laughed. "I've been reading up on hillbillies for the trip. I thought that was redneck foreplay."

I shook my head, more amused than peeved. "That's enough!" I pointed to my luggage. "There's my suitcase. Put it in your SUV."

"Geeze, Val," Tom mock-grumbled. "At least tantalizing Tammy delivered *her* demands with a side of honey."

Tom had hit a nerve. "Compare me to Tammy again and you're gonna feel the sting from the other end of that bee."

Tom grinned and reached out to hug me. "Come on, Val. Relax. I get it. You're afraid."

I bristled in his arms. "What? What would *I* be afraid of?"

Tom sighed. "Nothing. Forget it." He loosened his embrace. "Come on, let's go."

Tom grabbed my case and stepped outside. I frowned and locked the door behind me. Tom was right. I was afraid. All of a sudden I felt...*vulnerable*. Fragile even. As if I might be shattered by the slightest misspoken word. I took a deep breath and hoped Tom was right. I hoped there wasn't anything to be afraid of, and that I had been working myself up over nothing.

WHEN TOM PULLED UP in front of Jorge's house, the front yard was dotted with life-sized, semi-deflated holiday blow-up figures. A half-flat Frosty the Snowman hunched over the back end of a head-hanging Rudolf reindeer. I grinned and shook my head. *Leave it to the guys to somehow make even the holidays seem obscene.*

Tom climbed out of the SUV and rearranged the hatchback storage while I went to fetch Winky and Winnie. Goober answered when I rang the bell. The door's raised threshold added six inches to his already six-foot frame. I felt like a dwarf as he looked down at me.

"It's about time you got here," he said, his face twisted with sarcasm. "I'll finally be able to get some peace and quiet."

"What do you mean, Goober?"

"Winky and Winnie chose this morning to enthusiastically debate the sustainability of their ongoing relationship."

Movement caught my eye. Winky appeared from the hallway looking a little worse for wear. He shook his head. "Well, let it be noted, *I'm* ready on time. But I'm always havin' to wait on my alter eagle."

"What?" I asked.

"He means alter *ego*," Goober said, then let out the longest sigh I'd ever heard.

"What's an ego?" Winky asked.

"Something you got *waay* too much of," Winnie answered as she marched out of the bedroom dragging a suitcase. Winky shot her a scowl.

"Great," I said. "Two feuding hillbillies and I'm not even in Jackson County yet."

"Better you than me," Goober smirked and rubbed a hand over his bald pate. "Happy trails."

"As I recall, yore momma Glad weren't that far from redneck central herself," Winky said with a smart-alecky sneer. "She was from Kentucky, as memory serves."

"Yes," I hissed. "Come on. Let's go."

Crap on a cracker! I'd already been busted by a barnyard buffoon.

Not good, Val. You need to up your game if you're gonna survive the week in Greenville.

TOM'S SUV TRAVELED north on I-275. We'd just buzzed by the exit for Ocala when Winky popped the top on the plastic cooler I'd tucked on the floorboard in the middle of the back seat. The smell of spiced rum overpowered the passenger compartment.

"Whooowee! Smells like a whiskey bar at closing time," Winky bellowed.

Tom grinned at me and patted my thigh. I closed my book and craned my neck around to face the backseat. Up until now, Winky and Winnie had sat in the back in blessed silence. Like angry children, each had scooted as close as possible to their respective passenger doors and had pursed their lips until the blood had drained from them. Their lover's quarrel was my answered prayer. It had kept Winky's wildness in check, and saved me the trouble of having to dope him with Dramamine.

"What are you doing, Winky?" I asked.

"Lookin' for a cold drink. But all you got in here is a brick that smells like a booze factory."

"It's not a brick and you know it. It's another fruitcake."

Winky pried the lid off the cooler again and took another peek. He turned his nose up and shut the lid. "Yuck."

"I *like* fruitcake," Winnie said in my defense.

Winky shot her a look. "You *would* say that."

Winnie sneered at him, then offered me a smile. "You taking the fruitcake for you mom, Val?"

"Well, sort of. I made it for the competition."

"The competition?"

"Yeah." I sighed. "It's a family tradition. Every year, all the women in the family make a fruitcake. Then there's a taste-test. The winner gets a gift certificate for Jon-Boy's Pig Heaven Barbeque and gets to hold onto the trophy for a year."

"That sounds like fun," Winnie said. She took off her red-framed glasses and wiped them on her shirt.

"Not really," I answered sullenly. "My mother wins it every year."

Winnie popped her glasses back on her face. "She must have a super-good recipe, then." She sneered at Winky again. "I'd *love* to have it."

"I'd share it with you, Winnie, but my mother won't divulge her secret recipe to anyone. Not even Jesus. Besides, I'm not so sure it's her *recipe* that wins the contest as it is her *technique*."

"Her technique?" Winnie asked.

"Let me put it this way. The French didn't invent sabotage. My mother did."

Winnie looked startled. "What do you mean, Val?"

"Well, my mom likes to lower the odds. Last year, I'm pretty sure Mom filled Aunt Pansy's bottle of vanilla extract with soy sauce."

Winky snorted a laugh.

Winnie winced. "Oh my word!"

From the driver's seat, Tom chuckled to himself.

"That's only *one* example. Two years ago I caught her putting talcum powder in Aunt May's box of baking soda."

Winnie sighed and shook her head. "People is always putting salt in the sugar shakers at Davie's. What's wrong with people? Why would they do such a thing?"

Winky's eyes shifted guiltily. He stared out the window.

"I don't know," I answered. "But stuff like that is amateur hour compared to my mom. You'd be surprised what a drop or two of vinegar will do to a cake recipe. She got *me* with that one a couple of years ago."

"Geeze! Her own daughter!" Winnie stared in disbelief. "That's horrible, Val."

I shrugged. "Yeah. Mom never has been any good at putting her own needs second. But this time, I think I've got her beat. I made my fruitcake ahead of time. I figure with me and Tom watching the cooler, I've got a fighting chance to be the top fruitcake this year."

Tom snorted. I shot him a dirty look.

"Well, you've got my vote," Winnie said. "If it's the same as what you served last night, it's gotta win."

"Thanks, Winnie." I turned back to face Tom. He kept his eyes on the road.

Winky's cellphone buzzed. "What?" he bellowed into the phone. "Gaul-dang it! Uh huh. Well, I can't. I'm halfway to Lake City. You two's gonna have to fix it yourself." He clicked off the phone.

"What's going on?" Tom asked.

Winky frowned. "That was Jorge. He said something what'n set up right with the lights at the mayor's place."

"Oh. What's the problem?"

Winky tried to look serious, but couldn't pull it off. "It was s'posed to look like Santa on the chimbley, tossing presents down to the mayor." He grinned and couldn't stop giggling. "But Jorge said...*ha ha*...the lights was...*hee hee*...screwed up somehow...*ha ha ha!*" Winky lost his composure for a moment, then continued. "...and it looks like...*hee hee*...Santa's takin' a dump on the mayor's head!"

Chapter Seventeen

TOM STEERED THE SUV down the last exit ramp for Lake City. The juncture was the halfway point to my mother's place, and the drop-off point for Winky and Winnie. The plan was to have lunch together and wait for Winky's cousin Roger to pick them up.

"Where you guys want to eat?" Tom asked as he made a right toward an ugly lineup of chain restaurants and gas stations.

"I'd love me some Krystal burgers," Winky said.

"Sounds good to me," Tom replied. "Any objections?"

Winnie and I had none, so a few minutes later we were sitting around a high-top table for four, pulling delicious little steamed hamburger buns out of open-ended little cardboard boxes.

"Roger don't live but a few minutes from here," Winky said. "Val, can I use your phone to give him a call? I went and left mine in the SUV."

"Sure." I wiped my hands on a napkin and pulled my cellphone from my purse. Winky grabbed it with his greasy hands and punched in a number.

"Hey, Charlene. Roger there?"

"What? Uh huh. Uh huh. Well don't that beat all."

Winky clicked off the phone. "Dumb jerk went and shot hisself in the foot this time."

"What happened?" I asked.

"I just tole ya. Roger shot hisself in the foot. He was chasin' down a wild hog."

"Oh. So what does that mean?" I asked.

"It means he took his rifle and –"

"No! I mean is he still coming to get you?"

"Oh. I tole Charlene we was here. She said 'okay.' I figured that meant she was comin'."

"Maybe you should call her back, you know, to make sure."

"Can do." Winky looked at my phone and hit the camera button. "Cheese crackers," he said, and snapped a shot of Tom and me as I crammed half a burger in my mouth.

"Stop it!" I mumbled.

"Just commemoratin' this special event," Winky laughed.

I grabbed for my phone, but Winky was too fast. He scrolled through the photo gallery and waved around a picture of me stuffing my face. As everyone but me laughed, he swiped the screen and showed us a screen shot of last night, where I'd captured him gnawing on a turkey leg like Cro-Magnon man.

"Turnip boots is fair play, Val," he joked.

"Turnip what?" I asked.

Winky didn't respond. He was focused on his own image in the photo. "That shore was fun. Had us a big time, didn't we?" He elbowed Winnie, forgetting temporarily the two were feuding.

Winnie smiled. "Sure did, honeybunch. You want my fries?"

"Well ain't you a doodle bug." Winky grinned at Winnie, then lowered a waffle fry into his mouth like a crane. He hit redial on my phone. "Hey Charlene. You comin' to get us or what? Uh huh. Uh huh."

"So, you two made up?" I asked Winnie while Winky was talking to Charlene.

"Yeah. It usually doesn't take much to set things right between us."

Tom shot me a sarcastic grin. "Well, with that, I'm gonna go wash my hands, ladies."

Tom took off for the restroom. Winky clicked off my cellphone.

"You done with it?" I asked.

"Yep. Just one more thing." Winky went back to the photo gallery and started swiping through the photos. "Got to see what our little Val's been up to."

I grabbed for the phone. "That's none of your business!"

"Well I'll be horn-swoggled," Winky said. He stopped and stared at a picture.

"What?" I asked.

He showed the picture to Winnie. "Looky, there, if that ain't Mr. Peterson hisself."

Winnie nodded. "It sure is."

"Huh? Who's Mr. Peterson?" I asked.

"The guy who brought us the grill. To start our new, uh, cremation business." Winky held up a group photo that Officer Muller had taken at the police precinct party.

I nearly choked on a waffle fry. "Which one?" I asked.

Winky's fat, freckled finger landed on a smug-looking face in the crowd. It belonged to Hans Jergen.

I SAT SILENT AS A STONE in the seat beside Tom as we hurtled down Interstate 10 to my impending doom. Winky's cousin's wife, Charlene, had gotten a flat tire on the way to pick them up. We'd spent half the afternoon sorting out that mess. When we'd finally waved goodbye to them and they drove away in a rusted-out Chevy pickup, Tom and I were three hours behind schedule. I'd used the extra time on my hands to exponentially expand my anxiety, and to call my mother to let her know we were running late. After making sure I was well aware of all the inconvenience our delay had caused her, she'd grunted and hung up.

I was almost glad I had something else even more troubling to worry about.

Is Jergen behind Ha-Pet-Ly-Ever-After? Is that simply a pseudonym for his Pet Patrol business? I'd made Winky and Winnie promise not to say a word to Tom about Jergen. Not yet, anyway. I wanted to make sure it was true before I let the cat out of the bag. Heaven knows Tom and Jergen didn't need anything else to fight about.

I felt a pat on my thigh.

"Would you stop your worrying, Val?" Tom smiled. "I promise, it will all work out with your mom."

"And if it doesn't?"

"Hey, I've got wheels and a credit card."

I forced a smile and braced myself as the Quincy exit flew by. The next one would be ours.

"Fair warning, Tom. If you thought last night's supper was crazy, that was dinner with the Pope compared to what you're in for with my family."

Tom gave me a dubious look. "Why are you just telling me this *now?*"

I shot him a sly grin. "Because it's too late to turn back now."

IT WAS A FEW MINUTES past nine o'clock when Tom pulled his SUV up in front of my mother's house. The only light glowing in the rural darkness came from a solitary bulb on the front porch.

"Wait here," I said to Tom. "I'll try the doorknob to make sure she hasn't locked us out."

I crept across the yard and wiggled the knob, half hoping it wouldn't budge. It did. I signaled for Tom to come in. I cracked the door open and felt around in the dark living room for a lamp.

"Ragmuffin, is that you?" I heard my mother call.

"Yes."

"We done give up and went to bed."

"Okay. We'll see you in the morning."

"Don't you go sleepin' in the same bed with him."

"I won't."

Quiet as mice, I led Tom down to the bedroom in the hall, and found some extra sheets to make up the couch for myself. When I went to the bathroom, I found a turd in toilet. I tried not to read too much into it as I flushed and watched it circle the drain and disappear.

One day down. Three to go before Christmas.

Chapter Eighteen

I WOKE UP ON THE COUCH, half strangled by my flannel night-gown. Misty morning light was beginning to creep through the living room window in my mother's house. The shadowy shapes of heavy-legged pine tables and frill-trimmed lampshades loomed at me like *Dawn of the Doomed – The Country Décor Edition*.

I sighed and took in a lungful of familiar scents. *This is what home smells like*. I hauled myself to standing. A tinge of coolness in the morning air caught me by surprise. I'd forgotten how different the weather was in the Panhandle of Florida. In the dim light, I pilfered through my suitcase for a pair of jeans and a shirt with sleeves. I'd wiggled into them and put a pot of coffee on when I heard a voice behind me.

"Good morning, young lady."

I turned around. It was Dale Short, my mother's legally-blind husband. He was a sweet natured, slender, slip of a man. My sister Annie and I were sure our mother had hog-tied him and tricked him into marrying her. Thus we'd come to know him, love him, and nickname him, "The Hostage."

"Hi, Dale. You're looking well."

"I got no complaints," he grinned. "They don't fly round here, no-hows."

I grinned back. "I know *that's* right. Here's your coffee, just the way you like it."

The Hostage took a sip and grinned from ear to ear. "Ahhh! You always could make a good cup!"

Tom tiptoed down the hallway from his bedroom, fully dressed and groomed for the day. "Morning, Val," he whispered. "Good morning, Mr. Short. How are you?"

Dale looked up at Tom. The two shared expressions of mutual admiration as they shook hands. "Doing fine, son. You, too, by the looks of it."

"Thank you, sir. I am."

"Coffee?" I asked.

Tom looked relieved. "Yes, please." He turned back to Dale. "So what's on the agenda today, sir?"

The Hostage smiled. His eyes looked large and distorted behind the inch-thick lenses of his glasses. The dark, cat-eye frames were so old and out of date they were hip again.

"Well now, I thought you and me would rustle up some donuts from the IGA, if you're so inclined," Dale said with genuine pleasure. "You remember the drill, don't you son? We gotta get there early or old Tiny McMullen'll buy the whole store out."

"Sure. I remember," Tom said with a laugh. "Can I drive the golf cart this time?"

"Yessirre. After that I figured we'd go huntin.' Val's Uncle Jake ought to be by here in a little bit."

"Hunting?" Tom and I asked together.

"Yeah. Best to be long gone when Lucille's making that fruitcake," Dale explained. "She don't take kindly to no prying eyes about, if you know what I mean."

"That's true," I nodded.

"Val told me about the contest," Tom said. "Every year, her mom wins it. How does she do it?"

"I don't rightly know," Dale said, looking around warily. "She uses some secret ingredient can't nobody ever figure out. But I know. It's –"

Mom stumbled into the kitchen in her fuzzy pink bathrobe. I thought I saw Dale's heart darn near leap out of his chest. Apparently, she didn't overhear his last remark, because she allowed Dale to go on living.

"Where's *my* coffee?" she said in lieu of morning pleasantries.

"I'll get it," I said and turned to pour her a cup. "You guys can go get the do –"

When I turned back around, the guys were gone. The screen door slammed. Dust danced in glimmering in circles in the air current caused by their wake. I sighed and handed my mother her cup.

"Here you go, Mom."

"'Bout time," she grumbled and plopped her impressive rear end into her chair at the head of the dining room table.

"I guess I'll go into town and do some shopping this morning."

"What?" Mom scowled. "No. I need you here."

"But I thought you were going to make your fruitcake."

Mom eyed me with suspicion. "Who told you that?"

"The...uh...Dale."

Mom's eyes grew squinty with paranoia. "Huh. I hope he didn't go tellin' the whole world about it. People's always after my recipe, you know." Mom took a sip of her coffee and made a sour face. "I need more sugar."

The irony made me smile inside. "I know."

"What did you say?"

"I mean, I know people want your secret recipe." I took her cup over to the counter and added more sugar. "That's why I'm surprised you want me here. You've never asked me to help before."

"Well, this year's gonna be a little different."

"How?" I asked, handing her back her cup.

"You'll see."

Mom studied the newspaper while I studied her. Finally, I heard the golf cart roll up. The guys were back with the donuts.

"Y'all get my crullers?" Mom hollered through the wall. As if in reply, a car horn sounded from the yard. Mom's face grew red with anger. "I told yore Uncle Jake a hundred times not to honk his horn at us like we was common trash!"

Mom heaved herself from the chair. I followed her outside onto the porch. Tom and Dale stood by an old, rusty-red Ford pickup. Tom was holding a box of donuts while Dale spoke to a man in a cammo hat and shirt. The man was, of course, my Uncle Jake.

"Old fool," Mom spat, and waddled back toward the kitchen.

I walked out into the yard to hear what the men had to say.

"You bring ol' Daisy with you?" Dale asked Uncle Jake.

"Yep."

"Who's Daisy? A dog?" Tom asked.

"Nope. She's my good ol' reliable Mossberg shotgun." Uncle Jake pulled up a rifle. He pointed the barrel toward the roof of his truck cabin and patted the stock fondly.

"Oh," said Tom. "Why a Mossberg?"

"She's the best at takin' a full choke," Uncle Jake explained.

"Single-aught, number-eight buckshot?" Dale asked, then poked his glasses up higher on his nose.

"I figured ten, given our prey," said Jake.

"So, what are we hunting?" Tom asked. "Wild turkey?"

Both old men laughed out loud.

"Naw, son," Uncle Jake said. "We gonna shoot us down a Christmas tree."

Chapter Nineteen

AS TOM RODE OFF IN a dilapidated pickup truck to go shoot a Christmas tree with a legally blind Hostage and my unstable Uncle Jake, a twinge of panic shot through me. But it wasn't for Tom. It was for myself. I was now alone and defenseless against an armed and ready Lucille Jolly Short.

"Well, we best get to it." Mom rocked twice, then heaved her substantial girth up from her chair at the kitchen table. She smoothed her frizzy grey perm with one hand and sighed. She left her drained coffee cup and the empty donut box for me to deal with and waddled toward the pantry closet. As she fiddled around in the cupboard, from behind she looked like a fuzzy, pink grandmomma bear.

She pulled a sack of flour from the shelf and turned around. "I got enough ingredients you can make you one, too, Valiant."

"I don't need to, Mom. I already made my fruitcake."

Mom eyed me with her usual suspicion. "You did, now, did you? Let me see it."

I went out to Tom's SUV and fished the cake from the cooler. Mom stood in the open front door and watched me like a frizzy-haired hawk.

"Looks like a brick," she said as I walked up with it. "Lemme feel how heavy it is."

I handed the fruitcake to her. She unwrapped it and took a sniff.

"Dawson!" Mom yelled.

Confused, I turned to see an old blue tick hound come running up the driveway. I turned back around just in time to see my mother lob my fruitcake into the yard. The dog was on it in half a second.

"Mom!" I screeched. "Why'd you do that?"

"They's the new rules, Val. Can't nobody bring no already-made cake with 'em. You got to prove you done baked it yourself."

"But...."

"Come on now, let's get to it."

I gave my half-devoured fruitcake one last, forlorn glance, then followed the fuzzy pink cake-killer into the kitchen, as helpless and frustrated as a kid about to get a whupping for something she didn't do. Mom pointed a lazy finger at two pint-sized containers of candied fruit on the counter.

"Pick out all them green ones."

"What?"

"You heard me. Get all them green-colored ones out of the fruit."

"But...they all taste the *same*," I argued.

"I didn't ask for no commentary, missy. Your father, Justas, hated the green 'uns. It's cause a him I win every year."

I opened the lid of one of the containers. Plastic-looking neon-orange, red, yellow and green gelatinous globs shone back at me. "*That's* the secret? No green candied fruits?"

Mom sneered at me. "That ain't *exactly* what I said, now, was it?"

Sullen faced, I picked out the green chunks of fruit and tossed them in a bowl as my mother measured out flour and sugar to make two batches of batter.

"Now watch careful-like, Valiant, and do what I do." she said. I took my place in front of the kitchen counter, two feet to Mom's right, beside a mixing bowl and ingredients she'd set out for me to use.

"A cup and a half of self-rising flour," she said, and dumped it into her bowl.

I wet a fingertip and touched the flour Mom had measured out for me. I tasted the powder clinging to my finger. It was bland, dry and almost flavorless. I dumped it into the bowl.

"Add a half teaspoon a salt," Mom said.

I poured some salt and repeated my taste test. I looked over at Mom. She was grinning like a rotten jack o' lantern.

"Can't be too careful nowadays," she laughed. "Things can go bad sittin' on a shelf too long."

I was pouring half a teaspoon of vanilla into a measuring spoon when Mom dropped the bomb on me.

"I guess you heard Annie's datin' your ex-husband Ricky."

I steeled my nerves and didn't spill a drop. Disappointment flickered across her face. "Yeah," I said with all the nonchalance I could muster. "Tammy told me."

Mom's superiority complex skipped a beat. "When did you see Tammy?"

I stirred my batter casually. "She came to visit me last week. Didn't you know?"

Mom didn't say a word after that. She poured a cup of pecans on a cutting board and hacked away at them with the zeal of Lizzie Borden. In silence, we stirred our batters, added our fruits and nuts, and poured our batter into loaf pans. I popped both into the oven as Mom sulked and pretended to read the *Jackson County Gazette's* comics, or as she called them, the "funny papers." I dawdled around, taking my time to clean the kitchen so no "funny business" could go down on my poor, innocent fruitcake while it baked.

"When the guys get back from hunting, they're gonna be hungry, Mom. Do you have something planned for lunch?"

Mom looked up from her paper and grinned in a way that made me question my own personal safety.

"I got your favorite, Val. Look in the freezer."

I opened the freezer door, trying to hide my trepidation. Inside was a stack of chicken pot pies. If it had been a stack of dog crap, I would have been less aggravated. Mom didn't know with absolute certainty that I hated the taste of dog crap.

"*Pot pies?* Really, Mom? You *know* I hate them."

Mom looked to the left, her face a model of feigned innocence. "Oh. Is it *you* that hates 'em? I guess I got you mixed up with somebody else."

I wasn't falling for it. I knew it was a ploy to get me to go to IGA and leave her alone with my half-baked cake. *Nothing doing.* "That's okay. I'll call Tom and have him bring something back for me."

Trouble was, I had to fetch my cellphone from the back bedroom. I kept my eyes glued to Mom until my craning neck could stretch no more, then I ran down the hallway to Tom's bedroom. I grabbed my purse like a marathon baton and raced to the kitchen. I figured I'd been gone seven seconds tops. In that time, somehow my poor, feeble mother with the bad back and aching feet had managed to get up from her chair, cross the dining room and put on oven mitts. I caught her with those grubby mitts on the oven door.

"What are you doing?" I demanded.

"Checkin' on the cakes," she said, and smiled like an angel. "They's brownin' up nice. Have a look."

Guilt washed over me. I peeked inside the oven at the fruitcakes. "They smell good." I offered, along with a weak smile.

Mom eyed me like the resident evil genius she was. "Yep, Valiant. They sure do."

I FELT AS IF I'D AGED a year when the buzzer on the oven finally went off, announcing our fruitcakes were done.

"Happy birthday, Valiant," Mom said from her chair.

My skin crawled. *Could she read my mind?* "What do you mean, Mom?"

"It was your *real* birthday, yesterday, wat'n it?"

I'd forgotten all about it. When Justas had found me on the side of the road and convinced Lucille to keep me, Lucille had thought it would be funny to make my birthday April Fools' Day. When they'd gone to town hall and claimed I was their own flesh and blood, April 1 had been officially recorded on my birth certificate. Ever since, I'd celebrated my birthday on that day. But two years ago, I'd found out I'd actually been born on December 22nd of the previous year. Turned out, I was even older than I'd thought.

"Oh. Yeah. I guess you're right, Mom. Yesterday was my birthday."

"I didn't get you nothin.'"

"That's okay. I wasn't expecting anything."

I pulled the cakes out of the oven and set them on the stove top to cool. When I turned around, Mom was behind me. Her mouth opened as if she was going to say something, but the rusty creak of the screen door sounded instead.

"We're back!" Tom's voice called from the front of the house. "Smells good in here!"

"Did you stop by the Tater Shack?" I called back.

"Yes," Tom said as he walked into the kitchen. "Here's lunch." Tom dropped three large paper bags on the dining room table. His sea-green eyes shone with delight. "I'm going to go help Dale and Jake bring in the tree!"

"Oh! You found one!" I said.

My mother laughed. "Yeah, they ain't too hard to spot in all them woods, Valiant."

Tom gave me a sympathetic smile and disappeared out the door. I set plates around the table for lunch while Mom did her best to get in my way. I was pouring the tea when Tom and Dale came tromping in like two proud warriors, dragging the fragrant, six-foot long top of a pine tree behind them.

"Where you want this, Lucille?" Dale asked.

"Same place as always," she said, annoyed at being interrupted from reading the paper.

"We'll lean it in the corner for now," Dale said, "'til I can fetch the stand out of the attic."

Tom took hold of the tree top and stood it in the corner of the living room, next to my mother's hideous couch. Then he came up behind me and gave me a big hug. He whispered, "Miss me?" in my ear, then released his hold.

"Sure did."

Tom pointed at a dried-up fruitcake in the kitchen windowsill. "Is that your fruitcake?"

I sighed. "No. Mine's in a dog's stomach."

"What?"

I shook my head. "Not now. I'll tell you later."

"Then what's that?" he nodded toward the windowsill.

"It's the contest trophy. For winning the fruitcake competition. I told you Mom's had it since 1989. Well, it's been sitting in that windowsill the whole time. It's petrified."

"It looks like there's a piece missing out of it," Tom said.

"That's right," Dale piped up. He picked up the mummified fruitcake and held it two inches from his thick glasses. "That there's where Jake sawed off a piece back in '93. Darn near had to be hospitalized."

"What? That's crazy!" Tom said. His face was a confusion of disgust and bewilderment.

Dale shrugged. "Some people'd call it love."

"What do you mean?" Tom asked.

"Jake done it to smuggle a piece to his wife, May. So's she could figure out what the winning ingredients was. But Lucille caught him.

Made Jake swaller that rock-hard chunk whole before he could leave the kitchen."

Lucille looked up from her paper and laughed. "I sure did."

Tom turned to me for help, his expression too muddled to read.

I sighed. "I told you this was a competition, Tom. My relatives will do anything to get that trophy."

"But why? Excuse me, but it's...*ugly*."

"They don't want it for its looks, Tom," Mom said. "They want it for the *braggin' rights*. That trophy makes me queen of the family. I can't have nobody come steal it and find out my secret recipe, now can I?"

Tom looked like a deer in the headlights.

I smiled. "Congratulations, Tom. Now you know why Uncle Jake won't set foot in the house anymore."

A BIT OLDER AND WISER, after lunch Tom kept himself busy and out of Mom's way. He fetched the Christmas tree stand and a couple of boxes of decorations from the attic. He also helped Dale set up the tree in the corner of the living room. As for me, I kept an eye on my fruitcake. Once it had cooled down enough, I waited until my mother went to the restroom and set my plan in motion. I doused it good with spiced rum, wrapped it in plastic wrap, and hid it in the back of the closet in the spare bedroom where Tom was staying. When Mom came out and saw it was missing, she didn't say a word.

Later that evening, after washing up the dinner dishes together, Tom and I went for a long walk in the twilight. We held hands as we followed the twin ruts in the orange-clay road that passed by my mother's house.

"How are you holding up?" I asked Tom.

"Okay. You?"

"I'm kind of ashamed to admit it, but I feel *homesick*. That's weird, isn't it? To be here where I grew up, but feel somehow so far from home?"

"No, it's not weird at all."

"It's not?"

Tom hugged me to his chest. "You know the old saying, 'You can never go home.'"

"Yeah." I sighed. "Why is that?"

"I guess because home is never how we expect it to be, Val. What we think are memories are actually just ideas we've played over and over until we've idealized them in our minds."

"You mean like a fairytale?"

"Sort of. I've learned over my years of interviewing witnesses that memories can be faulty, no matter how much we believe they're true. So it stands to reason that home's never the way we remember it, Val, because it never really was that way to begin with."

"Huh. I never thought about it like that." I grinned up at Tom. "That's pretty deep for a cop."

Tom kissed me on the nose. "Besides, we *both* know who your *real* family is."

"Yeah." Those dang tears tried to fill my eyes again. It was becoming an annoying habit of late.

THE SKY HAD GROWN DARK by the time Tom and I arrived back at the house from our walk. Mom and Dale were stretched out in their twin recliners, watching their "programs" at an ear-splitting volume. Tom and I walked in and caught the last minute of *Let's Make a Deal*. A woman dressed like a lizard won a moped for having a boiled egg in her purse. As she jumped up and down with over-exuberance, Dale switched off the TV.

"Guess that's it for another day," he said. "Did y'all happen to see the dog when you was out?"

"No," Tom and I said together.

"He's been laid out on the front porch all day," Mom said.

"Somethin' wrong with Dawson?" Dale asked. "He didn't touch his supper."

Mom looked me dead in the eye. "Huh. I don't know what could 'a got into him."

Chapter Twenty

I WOKE UP ON THE COUCH feeling surprised I was still in one piece. *I survived a whole day at my mother's place. Just two more days to go before Christmas. I can do this!*

I rolled off the sofa and padded into the kitchen to make coffee. When I opened the pantry door, a box of cornflakes fell to the floor, giving my heart a jump-start for the morning. The cabinets, normally a somewhat-organized jumble, were in complete chaos. *Someone had rifled through the shelves.*

I thought about my fruitcake and grinned with smugness. Mom had done her best to track it down. But for once, I'd outwitted her. It was tucked safely away in the back of a closet, guarded overnight by a handsome cop. Even Tom himself didn't know he was on fruitcake security patrol. I was afraid my mother would find a way to pry the information out of him. I'd waited until Tom was showering last night to sneak into his bedroom and pour another quarter-cup of rum on the fugitive fruitcake. I looked up at the clock. It was now due for another basting....

I found the coffee and pulled open a drawer to get a spoon. *Geeze! Even the silverware was in disarray.* I got the coffee going, then fumbled around for flour, shortening and buttermilk. I whisked salt and baking powder into a cup of flour in a bowl, then worked in shortening by hand. As I poured dribs and drabs of buttermilk into the crumbly mix, I closed my eyes and "felt" for the right consistency, like my grandmother had taught me. Her kind, clear voice echoed in my head as I recalled her words; "You can measure things all you want, Valiant, but sometimes you got to go on feeling alone."

I worked the dough in the bowl until it felt right, then pinched off small handfuls and rounded them in my floury hands. I set them side by side in an old, battered baking tin made slick with a good smear of Crisco. I switched the oven on to preheat, left the biscuits on the counter to rise, and snuck down the hallway to Tom's room with a bottle of rum.

My hand was on the doorknob when it turned all by itself. The door flew open and Tom stood there, dressed for the day. He eyed me up and down, his eyebrows knitted together.

"What are you up to, Val? Come to wish me good morning?"

"Shhh! You'll wake them!"

Tom grabbed my arm and pulled me into the room. "I can kiss real quiet-like," he whispered, then proved it without a shadow of a doubt.

"Enough!" I gasped. "Don't start something you can't finish!"

"Who says I can't finish?"

"Me! Sorry, but the idea of my mother being in the next room is a real libido killer."

Tom laughed. "So, why did you come to my door with a bottle of booze?"

I glanced at the closet. "No reason."

Tom looked over at the closet and smiled. "Did you hide my Christmas present in there?"

"Huh? Oh. Yeah. So no peeking, mister."

I heard a toilet flush and panicked like a busted teenager. "I gotta get back to making breakfast. Wait in here two minutes before you come out."

Tom looked at me as if I'd lost my mind. "What?"

"Just do it."

Tom laughed. "Okay, Miss Fruitcake."

The first batch of fatback had begun to sizzle in the old iron skillet when I heard Tom's voice behind me. His hands rested on my waist.

"Yum, bacon! Have I told you lately that I love you?"

I twisted around and smirked. "Who are you talking to? Me or the bacon?"

Tom grinned and kissed me. "Can't I love *both* of you?"

"I'm not into threesomes," I sneered.

Tom kissed me on the neck. Instantly, I became as nervous as a blow-up doll in a room full of porcupines. "Stop! My mother could come out at any –"

"Mornin', you two love birds," Dale said. He rubbed his watery eyes with a handkerchief and settled his coke-bottle lensed glasses back down on his nose.

"Morning, Dale. Coffee?"

"Yes'm! You makin' your biscuits this morning?" he asked in a hopeful tone.

"Yes. And bacon."

Dale grinned. "Val, ain't you the purtiest angel this side of heaven."

Dale and Tom took seats at the breakfast table. I brought them each a cup of coffee. As I popped the biscuits in the oven, I listened in as Tom tried to make polite conversation.

"Dale, I mean, sir, have you got any more hunting plans on the agenda?"

"Nope. I could go in for a spot of fishin', though. How about you?"

Tom opened his mouth but my mother's voice came out.

"Nothing doing," Mom bellowed. She turned to me. "I smell something burning. You got the oven on, Valiant?"

"Yes. I'm baking bis –"

"Get outta my way!" Mom whizzed by me like a fuzzy, pink blur. She grabbed an oven mitt and yanked open the oven door. "Dang it, Val!" Mom grunted, then fished a meatloaf-shaped block of tin foil out of the smoking oven.

"Why's your fruitcake in there, Mom?" I asked.

Mom scowled and inspected the foil wrapping. "I don't need to explain myself to you, Valiant."

"Sorry." I scowled and placed the pan of biscuits in to bake. I grabbed my coffee from the counter and took a seat at the table next to Tom without pouring Mom a cup.

"Lucille, dear, why is it again we can't go fishing?" Dale asked, blinking up at her through his thick lenses.

Mom looked up from inspecting her fruitcake and shook her head like we were the most ignorant three people she'd seen since yesterday.

"How many times I got to tell you? We got *plans* for today, Dale. Now that the baking's done, we got to go make our cordial visits to the family."

"Oh." Dale said.

I leaned over and whispered in Tom's ear. "Translation, it's time to go size up the competition."

Chapter Twenty-One

TOM CUT THE IGNITION on his SUV in front of the run-down, brown-and-white doublewide trailer that belonged to Uncle Jake and Aunt May. They'd moved into it the year I'd graduated high school, and had done exactly $13.47 worth of maintenance since.

I knew this as a fact, because I'd been with them thirty years ago when they'd bought the trailer as a repo. The $13.47 was for a can of touch-up paint. Uncle Jake had bought it because he wanted to exactly match the turd-brown trim color that had been scratched in the move. He'd been grumbling about that price for almost three decades now, and it had become one of those useless bits of information etched into my memory banks forever.

"We're here," Dale said, in a bid to win the title of Mr. Obvious.

The four of us piled out of the 4Runner and waded through knee-high Bahia grass to the semi-rickety wooden steps tacked onto the front of the trailer. The steps had come with the property, and had been a stairway to nowhere in the middle of an empty lot until Uncle Jake had had the trailer placed so they led up to the front door.

Tom helped Mom up the steps while I knocked on the door. My knuckles made contact next to a wooden plaque branded with the grammatically incorrect salutation, "Welcome to the Marxs's Palace."

"Welcome to the 'House of Squalor' is more like it," Mom sneered.

"Now Lucille, be nice," Dale said.

I searched Mom's face for her usual 'drop-dead' evil glare, but it wasn't there. Her eyes moved back and forth, as if searching for something. I guess my knock wasn't loud enough. Dale came up beside me and rapped his knuckles hard on the door. A moment later, it cracked ajar. A pair of squinty eyes appeared in the crack, then the door flew wide open.

Aunt May stood there, arms open wide, all three-hundred pounds of her stuffed into a faded blue housedress. She shot Mom a split second of suspicious side eye, then grinned at me and gushed. "Yee haw! Val! I haven't seen you since the Pope pooped in the woods!"

I'd never gotten that analogy, but it was one of Aunt May's favorites. "Nice to see you, Aunt May! Don't you look pretty!"

Aunt May's plump cheeks blushed. She ran a hand through her silver curls. "Ain't you sweet!"

"Yep. Married life's been good for her constitution," Uncle Jake said as he came up behind her in a wife-beater t-shirt and a pair of dirty khakis held up by black suspenders. It appeared we'd interrupted him in the middle of either taking a nap or lapsing into a coma.

"Now don't start," Aunt May scolded him, "or I'll divorce you faster than a flea hopping on a jack rabbit."

Like I said, her analogies were pretty weird.

"Well, that's one promise I know you're good for," Uncle Jake said.

Everybody laughed except for Tom.

"Tom doesn't know the story," I explained.

Uncle Jakes face lit up. "Don't *he* now." Uncle Jake eyed Tom like fresh meat.

"Y'all come on in!" Aunt May offered with a wave of her hand. We followed her into the trailer and settled ourselves like dust onto an old, worn-out couch and a couple of armchairs, all aimed at a TV big enough to drive an ATV through. Hordes of disappointingly unattractive, beady-eyed relatives stared at us through glass panes inside cheap picture frames arranged haphazardly on cluttered bookshelves and accent tables.

We sat and stared at each other for a moment. Finally, Tom cleared his throat and broke the weird silence. "So, what's the story?"

"What story?" Aunt May asked.

"About the marriages?" he asked.

Uncle Jake grabbed Tom by the arm. "Well now, son, let me tell you."

I looked over at Mom. She rolled her eyes.

Uncle Jake settled his body into a chair and his mind into storytelling mode. "Once upon a time, Tom, me and my lovely bride Maysie got married in the Church of Our Free-Will Baptist Assembly Covenant Witnesses. Ain't that right, Maysie?"

Aunt May nodded her sizeable head, momentarily turning her double chin into a triple.

"Well, now, my Maysie liked being a bride so much she decided to make a habit of it."

Uncle Jake winked at Aunt May. Everybody laughed except Tom again.

"I don't get it," Tom said.

"Well now, we're kinda famous here in Jackson County," Uncle Jake said. "Over the years, we been married and divorced so many times we done filled out our entire punch card here in Florida."

Tom looked at me like a kid thrust onto the school bus alone for the first time. "What?"

"Here in Florida you can get yourself divorced as many times as you want," Aunt May explained, saving me the trouble. Besides, it was her story to tell. She smiled at Uncle Jake, revealing her missing bridge work. "I got me at lawyer in Marianna now that I got purty-well trained. He can do me a divorce in two days for $200 flat."

"That's the honest truth," Uncle Jake agreed pleasantly. "That feller even named a special after my Maysie. Ever time somebody asks me about gettin' them a quickie divorce, I tell 'em to call him up and ask for the Miss May special."

"Getting divorced is the easy part," Aunt May said. "But last time we went to the courthouse to get remarried, they told us that ten was the limit to how many times a body could enter the state of matrimony in the Sunshine State."

Tom's mouth fell open. I smiled to myself and watched his now mesmerized face change from horror to fascination back to horror again as Uncle Jake continued his story.

"So now," Uncle Jake said, and wiggled to the edge of his chair, "my Maysie don't like to take 'no' for no answer, do ya?" He winked at his bride.

She winked back. "Nope. I sure don't."

"So once Maysie got the notion we ought to get re-hitched, she done some asking around. That's when Clara Day at the Piggly Wiggly told her about a drive-thru weddin' place in Donaldsonville, Georgia. It ain't but about an hour from here, right, hon?"

"Yep," Aunt May nodded. "Gettin' married there's purty easy. We done been there what? Three times, Jake?"

"I'd say that was about right." Uncle Jack gave Tom's arm a friendly backhand. "Clever lady, huh? That's my Maysie."

Aunt May beamed with pride and looked around at each of us. Suddenly, her face fell. Her eyes honed back in on me. "Where's yore momma?"

I looked over at the chair she'd been sitting in. It was empty. "I don't know."

"Dad burn it!" Aunt May yelled. She rocked her ample torso to standing and pounded off in the direction of the kitchen, causing the whole trailer to shudder.

Tom, Dale, Uncle Jake and I sat and stared at each other like folks waiting around the ER for bad news.

"Lucille! Where are you?" Aunt May's voice bellowed out.

"I'm on the toilet!" she called back.

The four of us sighed in relief. Tom searched for something to say to Uncle Jake. "You look fit, sir. Do you work out?"

Uncle Jake laughed, then puffed out the scrawny chest hiding behind his stained t-shirt. "I walk near 'bouts four miles ever morning, young man."

"That's impressive for a guy your age," Tom said.

"Not really," Uncle Jake said with a grin. "The first two miles I walk purty steady, straight the heck away from here. Them other two miles is me heading back home when I done give up and decided I can't do no better than this."

Uncle Jake laughed and looked around the trailer as if surveilling his royal palace. Tom and I both smiled weakly, uncertain if he was joking or not. Aunt May hobbled back into the living room, suspicion still clouding her face. She opened the front door and an old Boston terrier hobbled in. "There you is, Teddy," she said to the dog.

The pooch wobbled over to Tom. He put a hand down to pet it.

"Careful there. Old Teddy ate my finger, once," Uncle Jake said. He held up a left hand missing its pinky.

Tom jerked his hand away from the dog.

"Oh my good lawd!" Uncle Jake hollered. He and Dale fell backward laughing.

Tom looked over at me, his eyes pleading for an answer. But I had no advise about how to respond. We both stared at the dog until Uncle Jake wiped tears from his eyes and reached down to pet Teddy himself.

"Well, it wasn't Teddy's fault, really," Uncle Jake explained. "You see, Tom, I sawed my finger off with my band saw. Old Teddy happened to be with me at the time." Uncle Jake reached down and scratched the dog's head, then spoke to him in the childish voice of a loving pet owner. "Old Teddy just loves him some table scraps, don't he?"

"Y'all hungry?" Aunt May asked. "I could fix us some lunch."

Uncle Jake looked up from petting Teddy. "Hey, Maysie, you got any more a them finger samwiches?"

The comment sent him, Dale and Aunt May into hysterics. As they laughed like a pack of wild hyena hillbillies, to my surprise, Tom joined right in.

Mom emerged from the bathroom. "You all laughing at me?"

The chuckles sputtered to silence.

"No, Mom," I said. "I was planning on taking you and Dale to lunch."

"Nonsense!" Aunt May replied. "Not when I got a big ol' package of baloney and a fresh loaf of Wonder bread."

"WHERE'S THAT SON A yours, Freddy?" Mom asked, her mouth full of ham, mayonnaise and white bread. Aunt May had fixed my mother's sandwich first, probably to keep her mouth shut and her nose out of her kitchen.

"He's a fruitcake, you know," Mom leaned in and whispered to Tom. Aunt May delivered my sandwich along with a dirty look for my mother.

"What did you say?" Aunt May asked Mom.

"Got your fruitcake ready for the competition?" Mom replied.

"Yes. I sure do," she answered and stuck her nose in the air. "And I got it put away for safekeeping."

"What's *that* supposed to mean?" Mom asked.

"Anybody who goes looking for it is gonna find herself on a wild goose chase," Aunt May said, and slapped a sandwich in front of Dale.

Uncle Jake eyed the sandwich. "You know, I was raised on wild goose chases, myself," he joked.

Really? I would have guessed Wild Turkey.

"Val, do you have your fruitcake ready?" Aunt May asked.

"I did, but I had to start over on account of the new rules."

"What new rules?" she asked, and put a sandwich in front of Tom.

"You're not allowed to bring one from home that can't be verified."

"What? Who told you that?"

Aunt May and I locked eyes, then turned and gave my mother a double dose of the evil eye.

"Where's my sammich?" Uncle Jake complained. "I'm starving, woman!" He got up and fetched a cardboard Advent calendar, popped open a compartment and ate the candy inside.

Aunt May slapped a sandwich in front of him. "You and that sweet tooth of yours! You gonna catch yourself sugar dibeetees."

Tom leaned over and whispered in my ear. "Are they *Jewish?*"

"No," I whispered back. "He's just in it for the candy."

"GOOD TO SEE YOU AGAIN, Val. Looks like you found yourself a fine feller, there," Aunt May said. She'd grabbed my forearm and pulled me aside as Mom, Tom and Dale made their way down the rickety porch steps into the knee-deep grass surrounding the trailer.

"Thanks, Aunt May." I gave her a hug.

"Now, I got two words of advice for you," she said, and put on her mother-knows-best expression.

"What's that, Aunt May?"

"The first is to always keep yore man guessing, honey. Like I do with Jake. Once a man knows he's got you for good, he has a tendency to lose interest."

"Oh." I pondered that thought for a moment. "And the second?"

Aunt May's eyes crinkled down to slits. "Don't trust your mama as far as you can tote her."

Chapter Twenty-Two

WITH BELLIES FULL OF baloney and white bread, we rode through the rural countryside on our way to my other aunt's place. Mom and Dale had passed out a few minutes into trip and were snoring like a pair of contented piglets. Either the gentle jogging of Tom's SUV had lulled them to sleep, or they were experiencing the onset of a sugar coma brought on by Aunt May's tooth-ache inspiring sweet tea.

As we passed the Rural Church of Lower Appalachian Apostle Witnesses, Tom shook his head. "Geeze. I think we've passed more churches than houses on this road. What's up with that?"

"In case you haven't noticed, this isn't exactly the city of brotherly love," I sneered. "Around here, wherever two or more are gathered in His name, there is *grudge*, not love."

"That's pretty cynical even for *you*, Val Fremden," Tom said.

I shrugged, then looked in the backseat to make sure Lucille was still asleep. She snuffled and turned her face to the window. "It's the truth, Tom," I said in a low voice. "You saw how my mom was with Aunt May. No love loss there."

Tom sighed. "I guess."

"I didn't tell you, but when I got up this morning, I found out Mom had searched the entire kitchen for my fruitcake. She wants to sabotage it, Tom. She can't stand the idea of anyone else – *not even her own daughter* – winning that stupid competition."

"I don't buy that, Val. If she wanted you to lose, why did she show you how to make her recipe yesterday?"

Tom's question short-circuited my argument. "I don't know." A dim lightbulb went off in my brain. "Wait a minute! The only thing that makes sense is.... Yes! Tom, the thing that makes Mom win every year...I bet good money it's not what's *in* the cake recipe, but what's *on* it. It's gotta be whatever *booze* she's using to douse it with!"

"Huh." Tom shot me a look that conveyed he was impressed. "That's a good theory, detective. You could be right. So where are we off to now?"

"Aunt Pansy and Uncle Popeye's."

Tom shook his head. "Where in the world do they get these names?"

I smirked. Poor Tom was a fish out of water, all right. "Popeye's a nickname. Pansy, on the other hand, is the real deal."

"Who are they? You're mom's brother or sister?"

I shot Tom an evil grin. He scrunched his eyebrows at me. "Don't you dare say 'both' Val!"

I laughed out loud. "They're the couple who spawned my lovely cousin, Tammy Jeeter."

"Oh."

Mom snorted so loud she woke herself up. She blinked her grouchy eyes and yelled, "Turn left here!"

I'd been so caught up in conversation I'd forgotten to give Tom directions.

"Valiant! Can't you do anything right?" Mom grumbled.

"Sorry, Mom." I bit my lip and stared at the road ahead.

ACCORDING TO MY MOTHER, Aunt Pansy and Uncle Popeye lived like "respectable folks" in a real house made of red clay bricks imported straight from Augusta, Georgia. After I'd missed that left turn,

Mom had fired me from my job as Tom's navigator and had commandeered both the SUV and the conversation. With barking commands, Mom directed Tom past the bottom of a hill to a narrow dirt road with the unfortunate name of Smelly Bottom Lane.

"That's the one," Mom said. She pointed a chubby finger at a brick house so spotless and blank it could only belong to someone with OCD or a severe mental disturbance. Not a bush blighted the borders of the house or yard with its unsightly green leaves. No messy potted flowers adorned the entryway. No welcome sign or mat gathered dust by the door. And the lawn was cut with such precision it might have been hand-trimmed with an electric shaver.

Knowing my Uncle Popeye, it probably had.

But despite the outward pretense of peaceful perfection, a legendary, long-standing battle of wills festered and boiled behind the quiet, brick façade. Aunt Pansy and Uncle Popeye were well known around Greenville as "The A-rab and the Shrew."

Aunt Pansy was slender, pale and frail-looking, but her flowery name and unassuming physique didn't fool anyone who truly knew her. If crossed, she could slice you to ribbons with her razor-sharp tongue before you could say, "How do." She also held grudges going back to before the invention of electricity.

Uncle Popeye's nickname was the biggest misnomer in Jackson County, short of Grand Ridge, a blip of a town with no "ridge" and absolutely nothing "grand" to speak of, unless you counted the one-and-only flashing yellow light at its intersection with Highway 90. The truth was, Uncle Popeye's eyeballs didn't protrude from his skull at all. Quite the opposite. His dark, beady eyes were sunk beneath a brow ridge so pronounced a seasoned rock climber would think twice about trying to scale it.

Of course, I didn't tell Tom any of this. I mean, how could I have? It was better that he figured it all out on his own. I knocked on the door and squeezed out a happy face.

"Why if it isn't little Vallie!" Aunt Pansy said with a smile that looked almost genuine.

"Who is it?" Uncle Popeye's voice sounded from inside the house.

Aunt Pansy's jolly face transformed into something dead and evil. Her head whirled halfway around like something out of a horror movie. "Why don't you get off your lazy behind and come find out for yourself?" she screeched at her husband. Her face then transformed again as she turned back to me and showed me that genuine replica of a smile.

"Y'all come on in!"

I took a tentative step across the threshold into their house of ill dispute. Aunt Pansy gave me a stiff hug as Tom, Mom and Dale wondered in like prisoners checking out their new cells and cellmates. Uncle Popeye emerged from the bathroom in a cloud of air freshener, filling the room with the aroma of rose petals dipped in manure.

"Caught me doin' my constitutional duty," he said merrily. "Woman, ain't you got no sense?" he griped at Aunt Pansy. He picked up the newspapers strewn all over the couch. His merry voice came back. "Y'all have a seat. Sit a spell."

We lined ourselves up along the overstuffed sofa upholstered in a plaid pattern that was outlawed for hideousness in 1978. All four of us sat on the edge of the cushions. There wasn't any use getting comfortable when a quick getaway might be required at any moment.

"Anybody want some sweet tea?" Aunt Pansy offered.

"Your tea is too sweet," Uncle Popeye complained. "I swear sometimes all you do is put a drop a water in a jar a cane syrup."

Aunt Pansy's smiling face went slack. "You best watch your tongue, Buford D. Jeeter."

For a split second, I wasn't sure who she was talking to. It was the first time I'd ever heard Uncle Popeye's real name.

"I'd love some tea," I said, to break the tension.

Uncle Popeye laughed and looked over at my mother. "You sure went and let yourself go, Lucille."

My mother's eyes turned to slits. "You calling me fat? Look in the mirror, Popeye. Chippendales ain't gonna be callin' you anytime soon."

I braced for a bar brawl, but then something unexpected happened. Mom and Uncle Popeye *started laughing*. I was so shocked, I sprang up from my seat as if I'd sat on a tack.

"I'll help you with the tea," I said to Aunt Pansy.

"Good girl."

I followed my aunt into the kitchen. As we fixed the drinks, I eavesdropped in on the "friendly banter" between Mom and Uncle Popeye that continued on in the adjacent living room.

"Don't be disrespecting me, Lucille Jolly Short." Uncle Popeye said. "I got a lot invested in this here belly!"

"You sure do," Mom said. "Whatever fifty kegs of beer cost. One of these days, Popeye, you're gonna run out of brain cells to kill off."

"You should know. It done happened to you."

The cordial laughter that followed left me shaking my head in wonder.

"You all right?" Aunt Pansy asked.

"Sure. I didn't realize those two got along. I thought they *hated* each other."

"There's more than one way to express your admiration, Val. Some people ain't comfortable saying things straight out. You gotta learn to read between the lines. Now help me carry the tea, would you?" Aunt Pansy smiled at me, grabbed three glasses of tea, then changed her face back to evil swamp monster mode.

"Popeye! You ain't got no manners at all!" Aunt Pansy screeched. "The only culture you got is growin' in your undershorts!"

Uncle Popeye sneered at Aunt Pansy, then addressed his captive audience. "Don't believe a word outta that crazy old woman's mouth. She's always ovary actin'...

Tom and I exchanged wide-eyed glances.

...'cause let's face it. Women folk just can't handle life without a man by their side."

That last remark proved to be one A-rab step too far for the Shrew. She blew by me and grabbed an iron skillet from on top of the stove. Uncle Popeye's beady eyes almost *did* pop out when he saw her. He flinched and blurted, "I got me a new pressure washer, fellers. Wanna see it?"

Before Aunt Pansy could take a swing, all three guys had disappeared out the door.

"Good riddance," Aunt Pansy said as the front door slammed. She set the tea glasses back on the kitchen counter and took a seat in Uncle Popeye's chair. I handed Mom a glass of tea.

"I guess he never forgive you for runnin' over his dog," Mom said.

Aunt Pansy shook her head. "Nope. But he's softened up some over the years."

Mom took a sip of her tea. "It could use a touch more sugar."

I sampled my glass. The overpowering sweetness set my teeth on edge.

"So what have you been up to, Vallie?" Aunt Pansy asked. "I haven't seen you in a month a Sundays."

"I was in Europe for seven years. Only been back a little over two years now. Things didn't work out with Friedrich, as you probably know."

Aunt Pansy glanced over at my mother. "Yes, I heard. But it looks like you got a new fella now. What's his name?"

With all the commotion, I'd forgotten to introduce Tom! "Oh! I'm sorry. His name is Tom Foreman."

"What's he do for a livin'?"

"He's a police officer. A lieutenant."

"Handsome lookin' devil," Aunt Pansy said, then flinched. "Oh, no offense. I didn't mean he was a devil or nothing."

I smiled. "I know."

"Y'all gonna get married?"

"I don't know. The idea kind of scares me, to be honest."

"Why ever for, child? You done been married now what? Four times?"

My face flushed with heat. "Three."

"No shame in that, Vallie," Aunt Pansy said unconvincingly.

"But you and Uncle Popeye...you've been married since you were kids."

Aunt Pansy smiled wryly. "Just 'cause it stuck don't mean it's all happily ever after."

"If you don't mind me asking, why *do* you stay together, Aunt Pansy? You two argue all the time."

"It suits us."

"Arguing *suits* you?"

Mom and Aunt Pansy exchanged knowing glances.

"When me and Lucille was growing up, our ma and pa fought like wild cats and stray dogs. Ain't that right, Lucille?"

Mom nodded. "Yep."

"But they was always there for each other. And we young'uns got used to it. We got 'broke in' to hearing a heap of fussing and fighting, like you do a pair a shoes, you know?"

I nodded.

"Well, after a while, the bickering felt normal. Good even. Like arguing all the time was all right. No. Better'n all right. Griping and complaining was just *the way it was*. Ma and Pa showed us it was *the right thing to do*." Aunt Pansy looked up. "Ain't that right, Lucille?"

We looked over where Mom had been sitting. Mom wasn't in the room.

Aunt Pansy's face turned to stone. "Lucille!" she yelled, then turned to me. "Dad-burn it! I can't believe that sorry sister of mine!"

Before Aunt Pansy could get up out of her chair, Mom reappeared and shot Aunt Pansy a smug look. "What?" She asked, her face a glorious imitation of redneck innocence. "I was putting more sugar in my tea."

Then Mom did something that made my gut drop four inches with guilt. She winked at me. Somehow I'd become a pawn in my mother's evil fruitcake-sabotage plan.

Aunt Pansy stood up. "Lucille, if I –"

"Mom?" The front door flew open and a familiar voice rang out again. "Mom, where are you?"

Aunt Pansy's unspoken threat hung suspended in the tense air, as footsteps clomped down the foyer. A second later, Tammy Jeeter stepped into view, wearing a short red dress that perfectly matched her shin-high cowboy boots.

Chapter Twenty-Three

"TAMMY, HONEY!" AUNT Pansy cried out. "You made it home for Christmas!"

"Hi, Mom." Tammy's greeting came out half-squelched as her mom hugged the stuffing out of her. "You know I wouldn't miss it for the world."

"Look who's here," Aunt Pansy said. She turned Tammy toward us for a better look. Tammy's smiling eyes dulled when they reached my face.

"Hi, Aunt Lucille. Hey, Val."

"Hey, Tammy."

"You drive over here all by your lonesome?" Aunt Pansy asked, taking Tammy's purse from her shoulder.

"No. I brought Rich with me."

"Rich? Who's that?"

Tammy eyed me with the same horror-movie grin she inherited from her mother. My face shot red-hot. I'd hoped to never see phallic-faced "Dick" again. I guess I could cross that wish off my Christmas list.

"Rich is a guy I met when I was staying with Val *all last week*, right Val?"

A confused smile crept across my lips. Then my embarrassment evaporated into anger. *I'm being played for an alibi – by the same hateful hick who stole my fruitcake!*

"Well, that's not exactly –" I began.

"Rich works for the mayor's office in St. Petersburg," Tammy said snottily, cutting me off.

"Ooooh, the mayor's office," cooed Aunt Pansy. "That sounds important. A lot more important than a *police lieutenant!*"

So that's how it was going to be, huh?

I looked over at my mother. She was settled into the sofa like a spectator waiting for a prize fight to begin. All that was missing was the popcorn.

Well, what the hell. Might as well give Mom a show. Never let it be said Val Fremden couldn't stoop to a challenge.

"It'll be nice to see *Dick*...I mean Rich...again," I said, my voice so sweet I almost gagged myself. "Did you enjoy the fruitcake, Tammy?"

Tammy glared at me and tapped a fake nail against her cheek.

"Just when exactly *did* you get back?" Mom asked to stir the pot.

Tammy forced a polite smile and directed her answer at my mother, but her evil eyes remained glued on me. "I stopped by your house yesterday, Aunt Lucille, but you weren't home."

My mind raced. *What? Could Tammy have been the one who rifled through the kitchen while we were out walking last night? Mom never locks her door....*

"Did you bring Rich with you?" Aunt Pansy asked.

"Yes. He's outside with the other fellas."

"Well then, go fetch him!" Aunt Pansy commanded, as if Tammy should have known better.

Tammy bit her lip, then turned and stomped toward the door. Aunt Pansy turned to Mom and me and said, "I'm gonna go freshen up." She hightailed it to the bathroom, hands already thrust in her hair, trying to poof it up. Mom and I were abandoned to our own devices.

"What did you mean by that fruitcake comment?" Mom asked when she was sure Aunt Pansy was out of earshot.

"When Tammy left my place, she stole my fruitcake. I'd been marinating it for weeks. The one you fed it to poor old Dawson was a replacement one. Probably the only reason that old hound's still alive."

"Huh," Mom grunted.

"Mom, you don't think Tammy will try to enter *my* cake in the competition?"

Mom stuck out her lower lip and shrugged. "I don't know. But it don't matter, Val. She can't win even if she does. Neither can her momma. I made sure of that." Mom smiled and patted her purse.

I shook my head. "Why does winning matter so much to you?"

"You saw them two. Ain't it obvious, Val? They think they's better than us."

The front door opened. Tammy's telltale clomping echoed across the floor. She stomped into the living room, dick-nosed Rich towering at her side.

When Mom spotted him, her eyes grew as big as poached eggs. She screamed, "Ah-wooo!" and slapped her hand over her own mouth.

Aunt Pansy came running out of the bathroom. "Lucille! What are you –" She caught a look at Rich's penile proboscis and her knees buckled. She fell backwards onto her scrawny butt, then scrambled to her feet, her face as red as raw hamburger. Tammy's expression convinced me she was prepared to chew through hardened steel.

"Why, welcome to our humble home," Aunt Pansy fumbled. She extended a hand toward Rich, but couldn't bring her Bible-thumping heart to look at his obscene face. When his hand touched hers, she flinched and closed her eyes, as if she'd been forced to pick up a human turd barehanded.

My mother, bless her evil little heart, started laughing. And laughing. And laughing some more. She didn't even stop after she'd gone and wet her pants. Tammy and Aunt Pansy looked as if they'd just lost their life savings.

"I think we need to go," I said. "Mom's had a little uh –"

Mom doubled over with laughter again and farted loud enough to rattle the windows. I grabbed her by the arm and pulled her toward the foyer. "We'll see you all at Christmas!" I said brightly, not daring to look in their faces. I yanked Mom out the front door. As soon as it slammed closed, I burst out laughing myself. Mom and I looked at each other and cracked up. Disabled by gut-splitting screams of laughter, we fell on our hands and knees, then rolled around in the precision-trimmed yard snorting until tears streamed from our eyes.

"You two okay?" Tom asked as he walked up to us.

"Yes," I managed between giggles. "But I think it's time for us to go."

Tom shook his head in wonderment. "What the heck happened?"

Mom sat up in the grass and gasped for air. "Tammy's always...had a thing... for *fruitcakes*." She fell backward again on the ground, laughing like a deranged chimpanzee.

Tom studied my mother. "Is she *drunk?*"

I stifled a smirk. "In a way, yeah. Help me get her in the car, Tom. I'll tell you all about it on the way home."

TOM HAD SCROUNGED A garbage bag from the back of his SUV for Mom's pee-butt to sit on. Exhausted from her laughing fit, she was soon snoring in the backseat as we bumped down the road, making our getaway from Smelly Bottom Lane. Poor Dale didn't last much longer than mom. Either he was bone-tired too, or the ammonia fumes had knocked him out cold.

"They're both asleep," I whispered. "Mom peed herself laughing at Tammy's boyfriend."

Tom grinned. "Really? I'd like to hear the joke that managed *that* feat."

"It wasn't a joke, Tom. It was...the way Rich *looked.*"

Tom shot me a curious look. "No offense, Val, but your family is no collection of beauty kings and queens. In fact, I'm not sure people like that should even be *breeding*."

I nodded in agreement. "I know. What can I say? My family tree's missing a bunch of branches. And as you've seen, they're not too particular when it comes to choosing a mate. I think having opposable thumbs may be enough to get a Jolly laid."

Tom grinned. "Well, it's a good thing, then, you're no blood relation."

"Yeah. But that's no guarantee of a good gene pool. You saw dick nose."

Tom's eyebrows scrunched together. "Dick nose?"

I stared at Tom, incredulous. "Don't tell me you didn't notice Dick's...I mean *Rich's* horrible schnoz!"

Tom twisted his lip and sighed. "Not really. I guess I was too distracted."

"What could be more distracting than a nose that looks like a pickled pecker?"

Tom didn't laugh. Instead, he hunched over and lowered his voice. "I overheard Dale talking to Popeye about his girlfriend, Mary Ann."

My eye-whites doubled. "Uncle Popeye's got a girlfriend?"

"No," Tom said. "Dale does."

THAT EVENING, ALL THROUGH supper, I stared at Dale, trying to imagine how the scrawny, blind-as-a-bat old man could have the energy to deal with two women – especially when one of them was Lucille Jolly. Part of me was impressed. Part of me was kind of glad for him – maybe Mary Ann treated him better. But the biggest part of me wanted to wring his neck. I forbade Tom to bring the topic up. I didn't want Mom to get hurt. I'd have to handle it later, when I could catch Dale alone.

After supper, Dale excused himself from the table and scurried out the front door. Mom waddled to the living room to watch TV. I was washing up the dishes with Tom when I saw Dale sneak by window into the side yard.

"Let's go for a walk," I said, pulling off my rubber gloves.

"What about the dishes?" Tom asked.

"We'll do them when we get back."

"But..."

I snatched the dishtowel from Tom's hand. "Just come with me, will you?"

Tom followed behind me, grinning. I bet he figured I was leading him off somewhere to have sex. I didn't bother to correct him. I tiptoed out of the house and snuck around to the side yard, where I'd seen Dale a few minutes before. But he was nowhere to be found.

"What are you looking for?" Tom asked with a cute, naughty grin. He pulled me to him.

I frowned. "Nothing. Never mind. Let go."

Tom let go of me and shot me a frustrated look. "Are you okay?"

"No!" I hissed. "How can you be so...*happy-go-lucky*, Tom? Why aren't you angry at Dale like I am?"

Tom's eyebrows met in the middle. "Wait a minute. You're mad at *me* because I'm not making myself miserable over *Dale?*"

"Well...yes!"

"That makes no sense, Val."

"It makes perfect sense to *me*. You're supposed to be on *my* side, Tom!"

"I *am* on your side. But if you can't see that for yourself, there's no way *I* can make you see it."

"Maybe you should go for a walk by yourself," I hissed.

Tom scowled. "Good idea. I think I will."

I watched Tom disappear down the dirt road. He never looked back.

"Good riddance," I mumbled to myself. But a pang of fear had taken hold of my heart like a vice grip. All of a sudden I felt completely and utterly alone.

Chapter Twenty-Four

PERHAPS TOM *had* been on my side all along, like he said. Why else would I have felt so abandoned and alone when he called my bluff and went walking by himself? I needed someone to help sort this out. A trusted friend to talk to. I snuck back in the house past Mom and Dale. They were watching their programs, oblivious to the rest of the world. I fetched my cellphone from my purse and snuck back outside.

I punched Milly's number, but got her answering machine. "Hi, you've reached Milly. I'm out having a fabulous time with my perfect, fun-loving boyfriend. Vance always knows the right thing to say and never disappoints me. Sorry, ladies, but I got the last perfect man. Leave your pathetic little name and number, and if I ever come off Cloud Nine, I might give you a ring."

Truth be told, Milly's *real* phone message simply said, "I can't get to the phone right now. Leave a message." The rest of the stuff was conjured up by my desperate, damaged ego.

Crap! I'd have to settle for Plan B. I punched in the number.

"Hi, Laverne."

"Hi there, honey!"

Laverne's simple-minded, cheerful voice sounded like an angel from heaven. "It's good to hear your voice. How are you doing, Laverne?"

"Oh, fine, sugar. The fellas have been coming by for lunch and helping me finish off the turkey and potatoes."

"Are they doing more work around your place?"

"Yes! Lord, everybody loves their rooftop lights! You wouldn't believe it, Val! Every night, it's like a convoy around here. People driving by our houses and takin' pictures. The guys even got a write-up in the *Beachcomber Busy Bee!*"

"Wow. What do you know!"

"I know *a lot*, Val. Thanks for asking! After the guys finished up the mayor's place, they got another job. Then a whole bunch more, like some kind of snowball, they said. They've been working around the neighborhood day and night. Oh! And I been plugging in your lights at night, like you said I could. I guess it's been good advertising for the fellas."

"Sounds like it."

"Hey. You don't sound so cheery, honey. Are you all right?"

"Not really."

"Tell me all about it, sugar."

"I don't want to bother you."

"Honey, there's no way you could ever bother me."

I thought about all the times I'd been petty and let *Laverne's* crazy antics bother *me*. "Thanks," I said and tried to brush off the guilt tapping on my shoulder.

"So, what's troubling you, honey?"

"It's Tom. We had a fight."

"About what?"

"That's just it. It was about nothing."

"Oh. Those are the most common kind. But they're *never* really about *nothing*, you know."

I thought about that for a moment. "It's all just too hard, Laverne."

"What's too hard?"

"*Relationships!* I'm just no good at them. I always end up feeling like I'm suffocating in a cloud of...*expectations*."

"Whose expectations, sugar?"

I thought about *that* for a moment, too. "Mostly my own, I guess."

"Uh huh," Laverne cooed.

"Why is it that I always want things from people that they don't have to give? I want them to do things they can't do...be things they aren't."

"That's natural, honey."

"It's natural to be disappointed in people? Laverne, I don't want to always have to lower my expectations. That would be *settling*...wouldn't it?"

"That's one way to look at it, sugar. Some people call it compromising. Some call it accepting somebody like they are."

"My Mom," I began, but my voice cracked.

"Uh huh," Laverne said, soft as a downy feather.

"I never have been able to meet her expectations, Laverne." A dam of pent-up emotions burst inside me. It took all I had in me not to cry. "My mother never *accepted* me. She *judged* me, Laverne. She *condemned* me. She made me feel like *I was always the one in the wrong*."

"Like you're doing now with Tom?"

Laverne's simple question cut through me like a hot knife through a warm dog turd.

Crap! "Yes. Oh my word, Laverne! How do I break the cycle? How do I *get out of this?*"

"Well, honey, that's why men invented alcohol."

It took me a moment to absorb that one. While Laverne waited on me, she giggled.

"I'm serious, Laverne! I don't want to go through life always feeling disappointed."

"I know you're serious, honey, but you don't have to be *angry*, too. Try to see the bright side of this."

I was about to tell her I wasn't angry. But that would have been a lie. "The *bright side?*"

"Yes, honey. I mean, you say you don't want to feel disappointed, so how *do* you want to feel?"

I swallowed a lump of anger. "How do I want to feel? I want to feel *satisfied*, Laverne. I want to feel *happy*."

"Well, good for you, honey! Cause you're the one with the key to your own happiness, you know."

I grunted out a jaded laugh. "Oh yeah? So, where do I find this magic key?"

"Well, I think you know by now it's not in the 'high expectations' drawer, right?"

I blew out a breath. "Right."

"The key isn't in lowering your expectations of folks, either."

I frowned over the phone. "Then where the hell is it, Laverne?"

"The key to happiness is in getting rid of your expectations altogether."

Anger shot through me again. "Geeze, Laverne! But then, people would –"

"Val," Laverne spoke up, cutting me off. "Who do you think loses when your expectations aren't met?"

"Whoever it is that hasn't done what I wanted them to."

Laverne laughed. "Maybe. For a moment. Then they get over it. But there's only one person who loses every time and for the rest of her life. You know who that is, don't you?"

Dang. "It's me."

"Like I said, we all hold the key to our own happiness."

"How'd you get so wise, Laverne?"

"A magician taught me that back in Vegas. Thank gosh-a-mighty, it's one trick I never forgot how to pull off."

Chapter Twenty-Five

EVERYONE IN THE JOLLY-Short household was hiding something. Mom was an unrepentant fruitcake saboteur. Dale was a secret philanderer. I was stashing my heart (and a boozy fruitcake) in a closet. And my sister Annie...she, herself had up and disappeared.

It was Christmas Eve morning, and I still hadn't heard hide nor hair from Annie, even though she lived only two miles from Mom. I hadn't confronted Dale about his girlfriend, Mary Ann, either. When I'd come back in from my phone call with Laverne last night, Dale had been snuggled like a bug into his chair next to Mom, watching TV like nothing was up. I'd been in the bathroom when Tom had gotten back from his walk. He'd stayed in his room and we'd both gone to sleep without speaking.

I sat up on the couch and yawned. Being on the outs with Tom had sapped my energy. I was about to turn over and try to go back to sleep when I heard a rustling sound coming from the kitchen. A shot of adrenaline had me wide awake in two seconds flat.

Either someone left Dawson inside, or Tammy was back! Or maybe someone else altogether was trying to destroy Mom's and my chances at the fruitcake competition....

The rustling sound repeated. I grabbed a cheap figurine of an old-fashioned outhouse off the coffee table and snuck into the kitchen. An unexpected, pink, fuzzy blur about scared the bejeesus out of me.

"Mornin' Val," Mom said. She put her coffee down, plopped into her chair and picked up the newspaper she'd been reading.

"What are you doing up so early?" I asked in a voice that had been frightened up an entire octave. My heartbeat thudded in my ears. I hid the figurine behind my back.

"IGA closes early on Christmas Eve, Valiant. It's a pure nuthouse every year. I sent Dale out to get the donuts a'for the store opened and they was all gone."

Something about my mother's tone seemed odd. It was lighter. Less sarcastic. It sounded...what was the word for it? *Friendly!* My heart skipped a beat. *Oh no! Is she going to tell me she's dying?*

"So why are *you* up?" I asked with trepidation.

Mom twisted her lip at me. "I didn't want you turnin' on the oven again, girl. You give me a fright, yesterday. I done put so much moonshine on that fruitcake, I was surprised you hadn't blowed us all to kingdom come."

"Moonshine?"

Mom bit her lip and looked down. She seemed angry with herself. "Dang it. Yeah."

"Is that your secret, Mom? How you win the competition every year?"

Mom sighed. Then she smiled begrudgingly, hoisted herself to standing, and opened the pantry door. She fished through the shelves and pulled out a bottle of castor oil.

"Castor oil? *That's* your secret ingredient?"

"No, Valiant! Don't be stupid! This here's your daddy Justas' moonshine. The last of it, I might add."

"But why is it –"

Mom looked at me as if she took pity on me for being so dimwitted. "Think about it. Whoever in their right mind would steal somebody's castor oil?" she said. "It's the safest place I could think of. But like I said, this is the last of it. When this bottle's used up, I can't make the winning fruitcake no more."

"Is that why you're telling me now? Because your secret doesn't matter anymore?"

The left half of Mom's face twitched into a grimace. "Partly."

"What's the other part?"

"The other part...let's see. How can I explain it?" Mom shuffled over to the table and sat down again. She blew out a breath before she spoke. "I guess it comes down to managing expectations, Valiant."

Laverne's words began to echo in my mind. Had my mother been eavesdropping on our phone call last night? "What do you mean, Mom?"

"People's come to expect me to be ornery and spiteful, Val. I know it. I been that way most a my life. But when Justas got sick and died, I give up caring about much a nothin'. I didn't want him to go, you know."

I hung my head, embarrassed, and nodded.

"I was mad at Justas – and even madder at God about it. I couldn't figure out no way on earth to be happy about life no more. It's been near-bout twenty years, now, and I still ain't forgiven either one of them sorry rascals for up and leaving me." Mom looked toward the kitchen window. "I guess what I'm trying to say is that *I know* I ain't been nice. But I *have* been *consistent*. There's a lot a comfort in knowing what to expect from someone. Even if it's not what you want. Ain't that right?"

"I...guess." I felt paralyzed and helpless, like a guilty child waiting for the inevitable swat on the backside and banishment to my room.

"Valiant, how many times would I have to say I'm sorry for the way I am? That I can't change? That the way I am *ain't got nothin' personal to do with you*. Would ten million times be enough?"

I couldn't look at her. My head was too heavy to move. "I don't know."

"Everybody at church talks about unconditional love, Val. It ain't possible. I never gave it, and I don't expect it in return."

A sudden fire in my belly gave me the strength to look Mom in the eye. "But you *do!* You expect *me* to be *perfect*, Mom! You pick me apart for *every little thing!*"

I searched for sorrow or remorse in Mom's face. There was none. Only defiance. And...*resolution.*

"I ain't saying you're wrong about that," she admitted. "What I'm saying is I never meant it *personal*. It's just the way I roll."

"Yeah. Like a steamroller," I hissed.

Mom stared at me, then snickered. "Yeah. I guess so."

"Could I hear it just once?" I heard myself say.

"Hear what?"

"The words. I'm sorry."

Mom sighed, then spoke as if she were announcing the weather for the day. "Sure, Ragmuffin. I'm sorry."

Horrific disappointment shot through me, as if the universe itself had answered my pleading question to the meaning of life, and it was, "Eat fiber to stay regular." This couldn't be all there was to this long-festering wound. There had to be more transcendence. More relief!"

"Feel better now?" Mom deadpanned.

The adult in me knew that my relationship with Lucille Jolly would never be the same again. The scared child in me was suddenly flat-out desperate for everything to go back to the way it was – to the familiar, the *expected*. Exactly as Mom had tried to explain....

"I don't know," I said. "I'd be lying to say it makes everything okay."

"I didn't expect it would. But Val, I'm not your enemy. Not like you think."

A wave of guilt threatened to drown me. All of a sudden, I wanted to confess my sins like a Baptist on Judgement Day. I ran up to my mom and knelt on my knees beside her. "I thought you wanted to ruin my fruitcake, Mom! I figured you were the one who rifled through the kitchen looking for it yesterday. But now, I think it was Tammy."

Mom laughed. "Nope. It was me all right. But I wasn't looking to ruin your cake, Val." She picked up the castor oil bottle. "I was gonna give it the last drops of Justas Juice. So's you could win. But you wouldn't know you'd won on account a me."

Either Mom was lying, or somewhere deep down inside all that sarcasm, Lucille Jolly Short had an actual heart. She'd shared her secret with me. Now I wanted to share mine with her.

"Mom, I think Dale is cheating on you."

Mom's smile dried up. She slammed the castor oil bottle on the table. "What do you mean?"

"Tom heard him talking to Uncle Popeye yesterday. About a woman named Mary Ann."

The front door opened. Mom's eyes shifted in that direction. "Dale Short! Is that you?" Mom yelled.

"Yes'm!"

"Get your hind end in this kitchen right this minute."

His small frame and slight stature made The Hostage seem excruciatingly vulnerable as he appeared in the kitchen, wiping sweat from the inch-thick lenses of his cat-eye glasses. I took a step toward him, hoping to shield him from what would surely be a lethal barrage by my mother. But no such attack came. Instead, Mom smiled up at Dale like a baby turtle.

"Did you get my crullers?"

Dale held up the box like a proud champion. "Got you the last two, darlin'."

Mom beamed. "Thanky. Oh, and Dale?"

"Yes'm?"

"Our Val here wants to meet Mary Ann."

Chapter Twenty-Six

I WAS SHOCKED TO DISCOVER how well my mother dealt with playing second fiddle to another woman. But I was even more shocked that Dale was still alive to tell the tale. He set the box of donuts on the breakfast table as I poured us all a round of coffee. Mom acted as if she couldn't care a flip about Dale's infidelity.

"I seen that feller with the funny nose drive by on my way home from IGA," Dale said as I handed him his cup.

"That's odd," I said. "Is Tammy staying around here somewhere?"

"Not as I know of," Dale said.

I looked over at Mom, but she simply smiled in a way that made my skin crawl. I guess the new, nicer Lucille Jolly Short was going to take some getting used to on my part.

"Should we wait for Tom?" Dale asked.

"Nope," Mom answered with a mouthful of cruller. "Let him sleep. He's our guest."

Dale reached across the table and grabbed the bottle of castor oil. "Oh, Dale, that's not the sugar," I said, thinking he couldn't see it clearly.

"I know. I been taking me a shot of castor oil now and again for years."

"What?" Mom said. A piece of cruller fell out of her mouth onto the table.

"It's good for you," Dale said. "That's what my mammy always told me."

Mom snatched the bottle from him. "Maybe so, but this castor oil's different."

Dale squinted at Mom through his thick lenses. "Lucille –"

"Morning, everybody!" Tom said. He strolled into the kitchen looking way too clean and shiny for his surroundings.

"Grab a cup of coffee," I said cheerfully, hoping to break the ice between him and me. "Dale got donuts."

Tom poured himself a cup and sat down. "Any glazed left?"

Dale passed Tom the box. He picked out a fat donut. As he bit into it, Mom timed her words for maximum choking effect.

"Eat up," she said. "Then Dale's gonna take you and Val to meet Mary Ann."

"YOU MIGHT WANT TO PUT on something nice," Mom told me as I rummaged through my suitcase. "Mary Ann is a particularly fussy one."

"I don't understand, Mom. How can you –"

"Y'all ready?" Dale asked.

Tom and I looked at each other, then shrugged. "I guess."

"Follow me, then," he said, and ambled out the door.

"You want me to drive?" Tom asked after him.

"That won't be necessary."

Tom, Mom and I followed Dale out into the yard. To my surprise, Dale went around to the side yard, as he'd done the night before when I'd tried to follow him. He walked up to the old garden shed and fiddled with a padlock as Tom and I exchanged semi-horrified stares.

"We keep Mary Ann locked up in here," Dale said, then flung the door open.

Mom, who was right behind me, started cackling like a laying hen. In the back of the shed, adjacent to a rusty old deep freezer, stood Mary Ann. She had a plastic milk jug for a head, topped with one of Mom's old wigs. Two pink, plastic funnels duct-taped to her drum-shaped body formed conical boobs. Two sets of copper tubes sprouted out on either side of her 30-gallon metal basin like spindly arms. Mary Ann was a moonshine still.

"Dale's been trying to recreate Justas' moonshine recipe for years," Mom said. "But somehow, it ain't never quite right."

"Y'all want a swaller?" Dale asked.

Tom turned to me, worried, and whispered, "I heard bad hooch can make you go blind."

"Yeah, but this must be okay because –" It suddenly dawned on me that perhaps Dale's afflicted eyesight had something to do with his penchant for moonshine. He squinted at me through his thick lenses.

"Try a sip, Val." He held up an old, cracked cup full of clear liquid. "This here's my latest batch."

"No thanks, Dale," I said.

He offered up the cup to Tom. "I'll pass, thanks."

"More for me, then," Dale said, and drank down the whole cupful.

MOM HUNG UP THE PHONE. "Your sister's coming to help decorate the tree."

My heart leapt up my throat. "I thought she wasn't in town," I fumbled. "She hasn't come by or anything."

"Well, she was out shopping all day yesterday in Dothan, with your ex, Ricky." Mom looked me square in my eye. "She's worried you might be mad about the whole Ricky thang, you know."

"I've been thinking about it. And it's all right, Mom. Ricky and I were no good together. Maybe they *will* be."

Mom smiled. "Well, good for you, thinkin' about it like that, Valiant. Don't do no good to think otherwise, no-how." Mom sighed and dusted her hands off, as if finishing the topic. "Now maybe we can have us a good Christmas, huh?"

"Sure."

"But first, Val, we need to finish up our fruitcakes for the contest tomorrow."

"Okay. But I'm curious, Mom. Why me?"

"What do you mean?"

"Why did you pass on your secret recipe to *me*...instead of Annie?"

Mom laughed. "Are you kidding? That girl couldn't cook a Pop Tart in a room full of toasters. No one would ever believe she could make a winning fruitcake on her own. But you, Valliant...well, to folks around here, yore some kind a international fancy person."

"I thought that was a *bad* thing."

"What? No! It means folks afear you, that's true. But more out of respect. Cause they know you can do anything you set yore mind to."

"Oh."

Mom winked. "Now, where'd Dale put that dang bottle of castor oil?"

Chapter Twenty-Seven

THE DIRT ON THE LIVING room rug dug into my knees as I knelt and pulled the tape off a dilapidated cardboard box labeled, "Kids X-mas." The sound of Mom's voice in the hallway caused me to freeze. She must have ambushed Tom as he came out of his bedroom. He'd gone in there to call to check up on the guys back in St. Pete.

"Lieutenant Foreman, just what are your intentions with my daughter?" Mom asked in a voice that implied he was up to no good. I knew that voice all too well.

Tom cleared his throat. "My intentions?"

"You gonna make an honest woman of her or not?"

"Oh. Err..I don't have to, ma'am. Val's one of the most honest people I know."

"That's not what I meant and you know it."

"Mrs. Short, what happens between Val and me is not entirely *up* to me, you know."

"That may be true, son. But a girl can't ask a boy to marry her."

My face flushed with embarrassment. Still, I craned my neck closer toward the voices.

"What? Marry? Um...well, why not?" Tom choked.

"Take my word for it, Tom. If a girl asks a boy to marry her, she'll spend the rest of her days wondering if that's what you really wanted, or if she trapped you into it."

"Why would you think that?"

"Because it's true. I learned it the hard way."

"Wait a minute...did you ask Dale to marry you, Mrs. Short?"

"What? No! I make a lot a mistakes, sonny, but not many of the same ones twiced."

"So, you asked Justas?"

Mom was silent for a moment. "Well, it was more like our hand was forced."

"Oh. Annie?"

"Yep. But don't you breathe a word of it to either of my girls, you hear?"

"Yes ma'am. Your secret's safe with me."

"Good. Now, do the right thing by my Val. Promise me."

"I promise."

A throbbing lump in my throat threatened to strangle me alive. As Tom walked into the living room, I turned and crouched over the box, pretending to study its contents, but all I could see was a pinkish-grey blur. Tom tapped me on the shoulder. A static charge sent sparks flying between us. But given our current spat, I didn't know if the electricity between us stemmed from romance or anger. I slowly turned to look up at Tom. His face was as red as a sun-ripened tomato.

"What are you doing?" he asked, his voice thick, his eyes trying to read mine.

"Decorations...tree...for trimming," I fumbled. My mind scrambled for something to say to erase the massive awkwardness. "Did you get in touch with the guys?"

Relief registered on Tom's face. "Yes. With Jorge. He said he'd been trying to call me all day about the Christmas lights they did for the mayor and you guys."

"Oh. Cell reception can be sketchy around here," I offered.

Tom stared at me with far-away eyes.

"Is everything all right, Tom?"

Tom focused back on me. "Oh. Yes. I mean, no. It turns out, the guys got another job on your street. But when they plugged all four houses in last night, it blew out a transformer."

"Oh, crap!"

"Yeah. Electricity's out in the whole neighborhood. And to top it off, the mayor can't find his dog. He was using one of those invisible, electric fences."

"Oh my word! What did you say to Jorge?"

Tom bit his lip and looked at me wistfully. "I told him it would probably be a good idea to skip town for a while."

And with that, Tom walked out the front door.

MY HEART SANK. I DIDN'T know how much Tom knew I knew, and how much he didn't know I knew. I wanted to chase after him, tell him.... *Tell him what, Val?* I blew out a frustrated breath. *You don't have time for this nonsense!* I scolded myself. *You've got to prepare yourself for the even bigger faceoff about to go down.*

My sister Annie was scheduled to arrive at any moment.

I needed to muster my best game face and most gracious attitude, and *now*. I looked down into the box labeled "Kids Xmas." What I found inside didn't fortify my position. Instead, it sent those pesky hot tears raining down my cheeks again.

Wrapped up like little treasures in faded yellow paper towels were every silly, shabby, and poorly constructed little ornament Annie and I had ever made at grade school and Sunday school class. Tatty, cotton-ball snowmen stared back at me with maniacal faces of embroidery thread and beads. Cracked and faded eggshell baubles still bore our childish scribbles of stars and bows. Twisted red-and-white pipe cleaners, once in the shape of candy canes, were now mal-formed and moth-ridden. But the crowning glory was a tragic baby Jesus made of walnut shells and elbow macaroni.

I sighed and wiped tears of sad and silly memories from my eyes with an old paper towel. Just when I'd needed all the emotional strength I could gather, I'd been reduced to rubble by globs of glitter and faded construction paper. I thought about heading to the kitchen for a dose of castor oil. But as I stood up, a familiar voice sounded behind me.

"Those were the days, weren't they?"

Chapter Twenty-Eight

MY BIG SISTER ANNIE towered over me just as she had when we were kids. I was on my knees in grubby sweatpants and a t-shirt. She, on the other hand, was wearing fashionable jeans, a cute Christmas sweater, and an unreadable smile.

Annie was a hairdresser by profession. Over the years, I'd seen her in every hairstyle that ever came down the fashion pipe, from short, blonde pixie to long, black extensions halfway down her back. But no matter what trend she'd chosen to follow, one thing had always remained the same – Annie's unintentional secret power over me. One look at Annie's immaculate hair, perfect makeup and trendy clothes was all it took to make me instantly feel like a frump-a-dump.

"Hi-ya, Sis," Annie said. She tilted her pretty, cinnamon-haired head and eyed me tentatively. "What 'cha doin' down there?"

"Hi, Annie," I said as I hoisted myself to standing.

We stood face-to-face in silence for a moment, taking each other in, testing the temperature of each other's temperament. We both knew this could go either way.

I tried to make my eyes smile along with my mouth. "Is Ricky with you?" I choked out. The words were meant as an ice breaker, but judging by Annie's reaction, they hit her like a ton of bricks.

"No," she winced. "I wanted to talk to you first. I want to explain...."

My worried brow melted with relief. There was a pretty good chance this wasn't going to end in a catfight. "Annie, you don't have to explain. What I mean, is, I'm *okay with it*."

Annie's face registered redneck astonishment. "Really?"

"Yeah, really. If Ricky is the guy who makes you happy, then I'm happy for you. Honest."

Annie grabbed me and hugged me tight. "Thank you, Val! I didn't do this to hurt you, you know."

"I know," I said, and hugged her back.

"He's a good guy, Val," Annie said, and released me from her arms.

I nodded. "He and I were idiots back then."

"We *all* were," Annie said, then laughed. Her forehead wrinkled. "So, you're sure it's all good?"

"Yeah. It's all good. But I have a confession of my own."

Annie braced for impact. "What?"

"Mom gave me her secret fruitcake recipe."

Annie laughed. "Oh, Val. Don't you know Mom by now? She walloped me with that whopper two days ago."

I shook my head. "I should have known."

Annie giggled, then mimicked Mom's voice; "Annie, you know it was for your own good. Nobody'd believe you could brew a decent pot of tea, much less make my famous fruitcake."

I smiled and suddenly felt fifty pounds lighter. "So, I guess that means we both ended up with a sort-of-sweet nut-loaf, huh?"

Annie laughed. "Yeah. I'd say that pretty much sums it up."

"WHERE'S MOM AND THE Hostage?" Annie asked as we decorated the tree together.

I unwrapped a tiny, felt elf that was missing an ear. "Tom took them out to visit Aunt May again. I think Mom's sabotage plans got interrupted when we were out there yesterday."

"Figures. Speaking of Tom, how are things going between you two?"

"Well, we had a little bit of a tiff last night."

"What about?"

I hung the hearing-disabled elf on the tree. Annie picked up a reindeer missing an antler and his back left leg.

"I dunno. It's Tom. He never gets mad about *anything*."

"That's a *good* thing, right?"

I blew out a frustrated breath. "You would think, Annie. But somehow, it makes me *mad* – that *he* doesn't get mad, I mean. Does that make me a jerk?"

"No," Annie answered, then grinned. "Apparently, it makes you *mad*."

Annie tossed the hobbled reindeer at me. It ricocheted off the side of my head, hit the outhouse figurine on the coffee table and knocked it over. For a moment, Annie and I were transported back in time forty years.

"Takes one to know one!" I screeched with laughter and flung the macaroni Jesus at her.

"Na-na-na-na-na!" Annie giggled. She dodged baby Jesus and flopped onto the couch. "I'm so glad you're okay with me and Ricky, Val. All this tension...it gave me a headache."

"Mom's out of aspirin," I said.

"How do you know?"

I smirked. "I've been here two days. I used it all up."

Annie chuckled. "What say we run up to IGA for more, then."

I turned my nose up. "I hate grocery shopping."

"Why?"

"I hate having to pick something. There's too many choices."

"That doesn't make any sense, Sis."

"Yes it does."

"How?"

"If I choose something, Annie, it means I can't have the other ones. I don't like narrowing down my options."

Annie's perfect eyebrows arched. "Well, that explains a lot."

"What do you mean?"

She grinned and shook her head. "Nothing. Listen. Come with me. It'll be fun. I need to get some polish remover, anyway."

"Do you mind driving? It's either that or the golf cart."

"The golf cart sounds like fun," Annie said, then patted her perfect coif. "If I hadn't just fixed my hair, I'd go for it." Annie shot me a sideways smirk. "But lucky for us, *we have options*. We can take my beautiful Ford Fiesta."

WE CLIMBED INTO ANNIE'S old Ford and were at IGA in three minutes flat. I'd forgotten she drove like a bat out of hell. As we pulled into the parking lot, I relaxed my death grip on the door handle. Annie looked over at a red truck. "Huh. Uncle Jake's here." She turned her head and stared at a grey, late-model Lincoln. "And Tabitha Barfield, too. How *convenient*."

"What are you talking about?"

Annie's pretty face clouded over with suspicion. "You'll see. Let's go."

I followed Annie into the IGA. Once inside, she walked in weird, hitched steps. Her brown eyes darted around the grocery store as we cautiously sidled our way down the cosmetics aisle. When we passed the baby wipes and rubbing alcohol, I took a double glance at an empty slot on the shelf. IGA was sold out of castor oil. When I looked back at Annie, she had a bottle in her hand. Her back was to me, and she was peeking around the corner of the aisle where the meat, eggs and dairy cases were. I tapped her on the shoulder. She jumped three inches.

"What are you doing?" I asked.

Annie waved the bottle in my face. "Buying nail polish remover," Annie whispered. "Shhh!"

"Why the sneaking around?"

"Look." She pointed down toward the buttermilk. "See that woman over there talking to Uncle Jake?"

A slight-built woman in her late sixties was chatting up Uncle Jake. Her face looked like an old potato, but her auburn hair, cut in a long, layered shag, looked fabulous. "Uh huh."

"That's Tabitha Barfield. Uncle Jake's looking pretty chummy with her, don't you think?"

I had to admit he was. "Yes. But surely they're not –"

"He thinks he can win her over with his charm!" Annie said, cutting me off. "Ha! It sure won't be with his wallet! Uncle Jake's too cheap to pay me for a decent haircut. Look at that horrible homemade disaster on top of his head!" Annie turned back to face me and crossed her arms. "I don't know exactly what the man's up to, but I guess it doesn't rightly matter."

"What are you talking about?"

Annie's eyes narrowed as her mouth crept into a grin. "I know her secret, Val. When it comes to Tabitha Barfield, I've got the ace of spades in the hole."

"Huh? I must be missing something, Annie. Who the hell is Tabitha Barfield?"

Annie looked at me as if I'd beamed down from planet Moronus. "Val! She's the judge of this year's Fruitcake Frenzy Competition!"

Chapter Twenty-Nine

WHEN ANNIE AND I GOT back from IGA, Tom's SUV was in the yard. I gulped down a wad of guilt and regret. I was anxious to set things right with him. But as we walked in the door, Mom informed us that Tom and Dale had gone out for a walk, and we needed to get busy making Christmas Eve dinner. I was setting the table when I heard the guys open the side door and tromp down the hall.

"Oh. We're only going to need five places, Val," Annie said as I laid down the sixth plate.

"Why? Ricky isn't coming?"

"No."

Tom and Dale walked in the dining room and nodded at Annie and me. We nodded back.

"Why not?"

Annie looked at Tom, then at me. She lowered her eyes and her voice. "I couldn't convince him you wouldn't cut his balls off and hang them on the tree."

I shot a glance at Tom. He made an "I told you so." face. I got mad again. This time, however, it was at myself. My reputation needed mending.

"You fellers get out of my dining room!" Mom bellowed as she waddled in. "Ain't there a game on or something?"

"I reckon," Dale said.

"Then go watch it. I'll have the girls bring y'all some tea."

175

IT WASN'T LONG BEFORE Mom had run Annie and me out of the kitchen, too. Me because I'd had the audacity to suggest making cranberry relish with real cranberries, and Annie because, well, she really *was* useless when it came to anything culinary. She and I bypassed the living room where Dale and Tom sat like zombies, worshiping their NFL god. We dusted off the dirty cushions on two wicker chairs out on the front porch and sat down.

"I'm sorry Ricky isn't coming on account of me," I apologized.

"It wasn't just you," Annie said. "He had an invitation to his daughter's place tonight. I told him to go."

"Ricky has a daughter?"

"Yeah. She's twenty-five."

"Wow. How come I never heard about her?"

"Because he just found out hisself this summer."

"Whoa. That's a big surprise."

"You should know. I guess finding out you weren't a real Jolly was a bit of a shocker."

"I guess, yeah. But somehow, I always felt I didn't fit in here."

"You and me, both."

I grinned at Annie in sympathy. "Why do you think Mom is so...so –?"

"Mom-like? I don't know."

"Why can't she love us like a normal mother?"

"What's normal, Val?"

"I dunno. Like on TV?"

Annie laughed. "Look around this dump, Val. Mom gave you the only thing of value she had to give. Her fruitcake recipe."

"Yeah. But only after she thought the secret ingredient was all used up."

"Still, it's the thought that counts."

"That's my whole point. What *was* her thought behind it, Annie?"

Annie ran her hands through her cinnamon hair and sighed. She turned to look me square in the eye. "Would you consider, Val, even for a second, that it was love?"

AS WE SAT AROUND THE dinner table that Christmas Eve night, I realized everyone looked different to me. They hadn't changed – only the way I saw them had. As Mom passed the sweet potatoes with little marshmallows melted on top, I realized she was right. She wasn't my enemy. As Dale pushed up his glasses and carved the ham, I understood he wasn't a hostage. As Annie served me my favorite crusty part of the peach cobbler, I remembered she wasn't my competition. She was my sister. And when Tom offered to clean up afterward, single-handedly, it finally became crystal clear to me why I felt so uncertain about him. I was afraid I wasn't good enough for him.

Tom deserved better than the likes of me, and it was time to let him go.

I waited until Annie went home and Mom and Dale were watching their TV programs, then I snuck into the kitchen to help Tom with the clean-up chores. He was standing at the sink, washing dishes and staring out the window into the dark sky.

"Let me help," I said. I grabbed a dish towel and a plate out of the drain board.

"You don't have to," he said with a sigh. "I've got this."

Something inside me snapped. I flung the plate to the floor. It shattered, but the sound was barely audible over the TV. Tom jumped back as I launched my final battle attack.

"Why are you so...so darn *good*, Tom?" I spat. "But more to the point, why the hell are you *still here?*"

Tom's eyes grew wide. "You don't want me here?"

It was a simple question, but to my mind, the answer was anything *but* simple. "I...I don't want you here if *you* don't want to be here."

Confusion crossed his handsome face. Tom's sea-green eyes turned grey. "What are you talking about, Val?"

"You've seen how bizarre my life is, Tom! My weird family. My odd-ball friends. All the wacked-out screwball stuff that happens to me!"

"Yeah. So?"

"So? So! Tom, you're so...freaking...*normal!* You deserve a normal life. You can't have that with me. I'm *not* normal. *I'm a freaking magnet for crazy crap!*"

Tom's face went blank. "So that's it," he said.

My heart sank. It was over between Tom and me. "Yes, that's it."

Tom shook his head and laughed. "And I thought it was me."

"What? What do you mean?"

"I thought you didn't want me."

"Tom! That's not it...don't you realize? You're *too good* for me!"

"Val, you truly *are* crazy!" Tom grabbed me and kissed me hard on the mouth. "I love you, you freaking nutcase!"

"But...but!"

Tom silenced me with another kiss. "Crazy crap happens, Val, with or without you."

"But...."

"You might think you're Valliant Stranger, conjurer of calamity, but you're not that powerful, Val. You're just a normal person. Like me. You don't have any control over what other people do. And you're not re-sponsible for their actions."

"And you're *okay* with me? The way I *am?*"

Tom hugged me tight. "More than okay. 'The way you are' is my fa-vorite thing about you."

Chapter Thirty

THE SOUND OF SOMEONE whispering in my ear pulled me out of a dream about Santa being stuck in a chimney with nothing but a sack full of fruitcakes for company.

"Tis the season to be Jolly!" someone said, and kissed me on the cheek. I cracked open a groggy eye. Tom was kneeling by the side of the couch, hair slicked back, fresh shaven, and grinning like a little kid. His crisp, red-plaid shirt was a bit too festive for my as-yet-un-caffeinated brain.

"Is that some kind of joke?" I grumbled, and pulled the sheet over my head. He laughed and yanked it back off.

"Don't be such a Grinch, Val. Merry Christmas."

I scowled, then tried unsuccessfully to turn it into a smile. "You're looking pretty dapper," I groused.

Tom pulled at a spot on his shirt above the pocket. "Like it? Your mom offered to press my shirt for me last night."

"Oh." I sat up on one elbow. "You know how that works, don't you?"

Tom's blond eyebrows met in the middle of his forehead. "Uh...she uses an iron?"

My lip curled upward like a cartoon villain. "Nope. Mom sits on it."

Tom's eyebrows flew up an inch. "Oh."

I laughed. "Believe it or not, it actually works. Hopefully, thought, she didn't engage the human steam option." I sniffed at Tom's shirt and crinkled my nose.

Tom's body grew stiff as a board. "Excuse me." He pulled himself up from kneeling and disappeared down the hallway.

"Sure," I called after him. "Merry Christmas!"

I crawled off the couch and padded to the kitchen, giggling the whole way. I had the coffee going when Tom reappeared, wearing a different shirt. I opened my mouth to say something, but Tom held up his hand. "Not a word about this is to be spoken of ever again."

I stifled a smirk. "How about I make it up to you with some biscuits and bacon?"

Tom sighed. "It's a start."

I laughed and handed Tom a cup of coffee. "You're gonna need your strength if you're gonna make it through today, Tom. The fruitcake competition starts at ten this morning. You can expect everybody to start piling in here around nine."

"How did this whole thing get started, Val?" Tom asked as he took a seat at the breakfast table.

"The Fruitcake Frenzy? By my grandpa's brother Ike, back in the '60s. He was a pastor, you know."

"A pastor? Really?"

"Yeah. I don't get it, either. I guess Ike figured there was no better way for our family to celebrate the birth of our Lord than with a cutthroat competition that always ended in tears."

AFTER BREAKFAST, I fetched my fruitcake out of the bedroom closet and gave it a last dose of spiced rum. As I patted it in, I spoke to it as if it were a baby. "I guess that's that, then, little fruitcake. Good luck, cutie pie."

"You seem pretty relaxed about the contest," Tom said.

"Yeah." I grinned. "Mom never found my cake. Plus, I'm taking your advice. I'm embracing the crazy. It's out of my control anyway."

Tom looked at me sideways. "I'm glad to hear that...I think."

I walked over and gave Tom a hug and a kiss. "So, how about you. Are *you* ready to embrace the crazy?"

Tom winked and pulled me closer. "I thought I already was."

I sneered. "Good one. But you ain't seen nothing, yet."

TO KEEP MOM FROM BOOBY-trapping the contest again like she had back in '94, the family had banished her from coming anywhere near the fruitcake holding area in the backyard. She also wasn't allowed to help set up the folding tables and chairs where the family's annual Christmas lunch buffet would be served right after the fruitcake judging. In fact, Mom wasn't allowed outside on Christmas Day, period, until Uncle Jake had given the all clear.

Having been a victim of my mother's meddling and sabotage myself, the family entrusted me to keep an eye on her while everyone else readied the grounds for the Family Fruitcake Frenzy. Uncle Jake, Uncle Popeye, Dale and Tom set up the tables, while all the womenfolk fretted over the decorations and, of course, their prize-hopeful contest entries. To be clear, "all the womenfolk" didn't include Annie and me. Annie couldn't cook. And I, of course, was stuck doing time as Mom's parole officer.

"I love me some pearled onions," Mom said as she put the casserole dish into the oven to bake. "Don't you?"

"I hate pearled onions, Mom. They're gross – like frog eggs and slime."

"I could a swore they was your favorite."

"They were *Ricky's* favorite, Mom."

"Oh yeah. That's right. Well, I guess he'll finally get to have 'em again."

"Can't wait. That ought to be fun." I put the finishing touches on a pan of cornbread dressing. "I'll pop this in the oven, too."

"Well, our work here is done," Mom said.

"Who's bringing the turkey this year?"

"Your Uncle Jake. He's makin' one a them fancy fried turkeys. I seen him setting up the deep fryer out back."

My eyebrows rose in horror. "You haven't been out there, have you?"

Mom shook her head and scowled. "No. Good grief, Val. Don't you trust your own ma?"

I said nothing, so I didn't have to lie. Mom studied my face with suspicion.

"Valliant, I just want to say this." She held out her hand for me to shake. "May the best fruitcake win."

I checked her hand to make sure it wasn't a trap. "Yes, Mom," I said as I shook her hand. "May the best fruitcake win."

AT FIVE MINUTES BEFORE nine, I received official notification that it was okay to release Mom to wander free. She and I toted our fruitcakes to the judging table and set them beside the other five cakes up for judging. Mom snorted with derision. "I see your cousin Darla made it again, this year."

I studied the other fruitcakes. The one labeled Aunt Pansy was shaped like a snowman. Green, candied-fruit eyes stared out from an otherwise blank face drowned in white frosting. Aunt May's fruitcake was round and long, like a log, with a tiny, toy saw stuck in the middle of it, as if forgotten by some miniscule, drunk lumberjack. Mom's and mine were nearly identical, and looked like twin meatloaves. The shiny, round cake with a hole in the center like a donut belonged to Cousin Tammy. The sorry-looking, lopsided lump of a cake was proffered by my Cousin Darla. The seventh cake on the table wasn't a true entry. It was the petrified trophy fruitcake Mom had held onto since 1989.

"Step away from the table, now, Lucille," Uncle Jake ordered. "You know the rules."

Mom turned her nose up. "Come on, Valliant. Nothin' worth hanging around here for."

I scanned the crowd for Tom. I saw him talking to Annie. When I walked over to them, Tom smiled and took my hand, then asked my sister a question. "Why don't you have a cake in the running, Annie?"

"Annie doesn't like to compete," I said, saving her from having to explain her abysmal lack of culinary skills.

Annie smiled and winked at me. "She's right. I don't like to compete. Not with family, anyway. It never ends well."

"Where's Ricky?" I asked.

"Delayed," Annie said. "He –"

Uncle Jakes booming voice cut her off. "All contestants in the Fruitcake Frenzy are now invited to step forward and make all final preparations," he blasted through a megaphone like a NASCAR announcer.

"Here we go," Annie said, and elbowed Tom.

"Good luck," Tom said, and kissed me.

"Luck's got nothing to do with it," Annie said.

All six of us competitors lined up for last-minute preps and to unveil our secret weapons. First up was Aunt Pansy. She pulled out a bottle of Maraschino cherries and placed them in a crescent below the green fruit eyes on the snowman face. "A winning smile!" she said haughtily. The crowd broke out into scattered applause. "Go Pansy!" Uncle Popeye yelled.

"Amateur," Mom snorted.

Second up was Cousin Darla. She, lord help her, buried her horrible lumpy fruitcake in carrot-and-raisin salad. It was a stroke of genius. She'd figured out the only way on earth to make her gross cake look even worse. Mom snickered so hard she had to cross her legs to keep from pissing her pants. Not a single one of us clapped or uttered a word.

Third at bat was Aunt May. She added clumps of green holly made from sugar icing around her log-shaped cake. "Mighty purty, I might say!" Uncle Jake said over the blow-horn. Half a dozen people nodded and clapped.

Mom turned to me and whispered, "Three down, one to go."

Tammy stepped in front of her donut-shaped cake and gave Mom the skank eye. She pulled out a bottle of castor oil, doused her cake with it, and looked around proudly. I heard Aunt Pansy gasp.

"What a chump," Mom said under her breath.

I was up next. Stage fright rendered me weak in the knees. I wobbled up to my cake and pulled out a miniature bottle of spiced rum. When I went to open it, I realized the seal had been broken. I held the bottle up to the sunlight. The color was wrong. I shot Mom a glance. She looked away, her innocent nose three inches higher.

Panic shot through me. *Is this the last of my father's moonshine? Was she not lying earlier? Does Mom actually want me to win? But wait! What if it's castor oil! Or baby lotion? Should I pour it on anyway, and let my mother have her last victory?* I hesitated for one final second, then made my decision.

No!

I pretended to fumble with the bottle. I dropped it onto the ground and watched its contents pour out onto the ground. I searched Mom's face for a reaction. All I could garner for sure was disappointment. I forced a smile at the crowd.

"Well, good thing my cake is perfect just the way it is," I said. Tom and Annie cheered as I relinquished the stage to the reigning Queen. *Let her do her worst.*

Mom stepped up and poured a colorless liquid over her cake. The crowd was dead silent, except for one hillbilly hoot from Dale. Mom eyed the audience like a shepherdess does her sheep.

"That ends the preparation round," blasted Uncle Jake's voice. "May the best fruitcake win! Now, fine folks, without further ado, will our honored judge, Miss Tabitha Barfield, please approach the cake table!"

We all looked around, but Tabitha was nowhere to be found.

Uncle Popeye hollered out, "She just called. Said she's got a flat."

Chapter Thirty-One

I STOMPED BEHIND MOM like a scolded child as she wobbled her way across the yard to where Annie, Dale and Tom were standing.

"Why did you try to ruin my fruitcake?" I hissed behind her.

"I didn't do no such thang," Mom said. "I want you to carry on my legacy."

"A legacy of cheating? No thanks!"

Mom stopped and turned around, calling my bluff. I shrunk back from her, red-faced.

"It ain't cheatin', Val. It's sizin' up the competition."

"Here she comes," Uncle Jake yelled on the blow horn.

We all turned our heads as a red Camaro pulled up along the side of the house and rolled halfway into the backyard. A beer-bellied redneck in an old Johnny Cash t-shirt and jeans flung open a door and hauled himself out. I squinted for a clearer look and my jaw went slack. Ricky sure had let himself go. Not a hint of jealousy or remorse came over me. The only thought I had was that I hoped he'd be good to my sister Annie.

Ricky went around to the passenger side of the Camaro and opened the door. A slender old lady with great hair and a face like a lump of raw dough got out and stood up. Tabitha Barfield had arrived. She walked through the crowd, nodding like a politician and a beauty queen rolled into one. In one hand she carried a notepad that would soon seal our fate for another year.

"I wonder why she's so late," Mom pondered, her eyes as narrow as slits.

"She had a flat," I said.

"Flat my behind."

Mom and I had picked our way across the yard to where Annie, Dale and Tom were standing just as Ricky came up. He kissed Annie on the cheek, then turned to me and said, "Howdy, Val."

I nodded. "Howdy, Ricky."

I braced for the inevitable questions, but none came. Instead, Ricky turned to Mom and asked, "So, who you think is gonna win, Mrs. Short?"

Mom smirked. "Why, me a course."

Ricky laughed the easy way I remembered from decades past. "How can you be so sure?"

"She has her ways, don't you Mom?" Annie said.

Mom grinned and took her position as star of the show. "Now y'all, I can't help it if your Aunt May don't know the difference between condensed milk and Elmer's glue."

Annie's eyes widened. "You didn't!"

Mom plastered on her signature evil grin. "Now don't go blamin' me for nothin'. I wasn't the one what put the glue in her cake. *She* did."

"And Aunt Pansy?" I asked.

"Well, let's just say Elmer's can also be mistaken for half-n-half when you're making icing."

"Diabolical!" Annie shook her head. Dale, Tom and Ricky laughed.

"What about Darla?" I asked.

"Ain't never no need to do nothin' there," Mom said. "Look at her."

We all glanced over at Cousin Darla. She was prancing around in a loose-flowing, tie-dyed dress and an oversized, baggy sweater that still resembled whatever animal had given up its hair to make it.

"She's a dang old hippy vegan!" Mom spat.

"So?" I asked. "What's wrong with that?"

Mom shook her head. "Goes against nature. 'Specially 'round here. Darla don't never stand a chance. It's *Tammy* what's the wildcard. But I fixed her wagon good this year. Or more like it, I helped her fix her own wagon."

"What do you mean?" I asked.

"I seen that old boy with the funny nose peekin' in the kitchen winder the other day, when I was showin' you my secret recipe, Val. So, I put on a little show. It's a free country. I can do what I want in my own house."

"I don't get it."

"The castor oil!" Mom said. "I knowed he was watchin, but he couldn't hear what we was sayin'. So I pertended that's what the secret to my recipe was. I made that big deal a showin' you how I put it on the cake and all."

"But...."

"Now, what that feller *done* with that information was none of my business."

"So, you're saying Tammy sabotaged herself?"

Mom grinned. "You can't fix stupid. But you can usually count on stupid to fix itself."

"Let the Tastin' Commence!" Uncle Jake's voice boomed over the megaphone.

We all watched in paralytic anticipation as Tabitha Barfield prepared to take a bite from each cake. First up was Aunt Pansy's snowman. Tabitha tried her darnedest to cut through the dried-glue icing with a serrated knife, but couldn't make a scratch. After several attempts, she gave up, turned the cake over and forked out a piece from the underside. She held it up to her mouth, grimaced, and took a nibble. Her face softened into thoughtfulness as she chewed. She put the cake down and wrote something on her notepad.

I looked over at Mom. Her eyes were squints of evil. Her pursed lips stuck out far enough for her to kiss someone through a picket fence. She grunted as Tabitha moved on to Cousin Darla's carrot-raisin heap.

Tabitha fought back a gag as she cut herself a piece of cake roughly the size of two molecules. She put the infinitesimal morsel on the tip of her tongue for one second, smiled weakly, then pretending to wipe her lips with a napkin. But we all saw it. She wiped her tongue instead. She made a quick entry in her notepad.

Mom's cake came next. Tabitha cut a slice and put a forkful in her mouth. She chewed, smiled and nodded at Mom. Suddenly, Tabitha frowned. The old woman opened her mouth and pulled something out. She shook her head and held the object up for the crowd to see. It was a piece of pecan shell!

The crowd began to buzz like a hive of killer bees. It was anyone's game now! Tabitha turned her back to the crowd and scribbled in her notepad.

Mom shot me some majorly evil side eye.

"What?" I asked, incredulous. "You think *I* did that?"

Mom's face softened and paled. "Dale, get me a chair," she whispered, "I feel faint."

Next came Tammy's cake. Tabitha cut a small slice and put a forkful to her lips, then stopped. She sniffed the cake. Her nose crinkled. The old woman put the forkful down and divided it in half with her fork. She started to lift the smaller piece, but changed her mind midstream. She lowered it and divided the small portion of cake yet again. Finally, Tabitha put the cake to her trembling lips. She closed her eyes, grimaced and shoved the cake in her mouth. She chewed twice, made a sour face and swallowed. Mom snickered as Tabitha wrote feverishly in her judge's notebook.

Aunt May's log cake was up next. It truly was a beautiful entry. Tabitha smiled at Aunt May and gave her a thumb's up. For fun, she tried to move the little saw up and down, but it wouldn't budge. Her face turned from amused to appalled, and she looked squarely at Mom. Tabitha got out the serrated knife again, but no matter which way she turned the cake, the old woman couldn't get a knife in it. She scribbled a quick entry in her notebook.

My cake was the remaining contest entry. I held my breath as Tabitha cut into it. She raised a forkful to her nose and sniffed it tenuously. Her face softened with relief. She took a bite and chewed it for a second. Pride washed over me when she looked my way and smiled. But the feeling was short-lived, because right after that, Tabitha Barfield did something odd. She turned and gave Uncle Jake an ever-so-subtle wink.

"She's up to something," I said aloud as Tabitha scribbled in her notebook.

"I'm on it," Annie said, and made a beeline for Miss Barfield.

"I'm right behind you."

"YOUR MOM'S UP TO HER tricks again," Tabitha Barfield said as we approached.

"Maybe. But we've got nothing to do with it," I said.

"Well, what's done is done," she sneered.

Annie eyed her up and down. "Tabitha, all I'm saying is this better be a fair fight."

"I have every intention of making it that," Tabitha said haughtily.

"You better," Annie growled with the hardened face of a drill Sargent. "'Cause if you don't, Tabitha, I'm gonna snatch you ball-headed and never fix you up a good wig again!"

Tabitha's eyes doubled and she shrunk back in horror. "You wouldn't!"

"You just go ahead and try me."

Tabitha's face turned as pale and lumpy as Tom's mashed potatoes.

"So. We understand each other?" Annie asked.

"Yes." Tabitha said.

Annie's hard face snapped back to its usual sweet, Southern mode. "Well good. I'm glad to hear it. I'll see you at the beauty shop Wednesday, then."

Tabitha nodded and smiled wanly. "Yes."

"That's a wig?" I asked as we walked back toward where the others were waiting.

"Val, please!" Annie said. "Nobody's got *real* hair that looks that good."

"So, the competition's over?" Tom asked as we walked up.

Annie and I laughed.

"Oh no, Tommy boy," Annie said. "It's just begun."

Chapter Thirty-Two

"SO, WHAT'S NEXT?" TOM asked as he carried the cornbread stuffing outside to the buffet table.

"Dinner and a show," I answered.

"What kind of show?"

"A hillbilly mow-down."

"You mean hoedown?"

"Nope."

Tom shot me a sideways glance. "Can this day get any worse?"

"You heard my mother, Tom. She's cooked everybody's goose – *and they know it*. What's good for the goose don't always turn out so good for the gander."

"Geeze!" Tom said. "What do we do now?"

"My advice? Keep your head low. And don't eat the pearled onions."

Tom crinkled his nose. "I wasn't planning on it. They're disgusting."

I grinned. "I knew there was something I liked about you."

I handed Tom a glass of iced tea. "Let's sit back and enjoy the show."

I led Tom to the epicenter of the action – the seat across the table from my Mom. We'd barely settled in our seats when Tammy Jeeter came clomping up carrying two paper grocery sacks. One said Publix, the other IGA.

"You can have all this," Tammy hissed, and thrust the Publix bag at me. "I won't be needing it anymore." The bag toppled over. A bottle of spiced rum fell out and rolled in front of me.

"What?" I asked, confused. "Wait...did you buy this –"

"And as for *you*," Tammy shrieked, "Aunt Lucille, well...*screw you!*" Tammy slammed the IGA bag down on the table. Bottles of castor oil inside clinked together pretty melodiously, considering the circumstances.

"Thanks all the same, Tammy," Mom grinned. "But as you probably figured out by now, I don't have no use for no castor oil."

"Arrrgh!" Tammy ground her teeth as Mom laid it on thicker.

"Tammy dear, just seein' you looking so happy puts a smile on my face. Now where's that boyfriend of yours? Dick, was it?"

"*Rich!*" Tammy screeched. *Rich!*" Tammy stuck her nose in the air. "He had to leave. There was an emergency at the mayor's place."

"The mayor's office! That's purty high-falutin!" Mom said. "He must be darn important, then."

"He is!" shouted Tammy. "He was called by the mayor himself. They needed him on account of some dire circumcisions." Tammy's upturned nose took a downward dive. "I mean...*circumstances!*"

Mom burst out laughing. Tammy looked at me. "I feel sorry for you, Val. Having that monster for a momma!" She stomped off.

I opened my mouth to say something, but Tom grabbed me by the arm. "Did you hear her? An emergency at the mayor's?"

"You don't think –"

"I better go make a call," Tom said, "just to make sure."

I nodded. Tom got up and left. Mom eyed me with a holier-than-though look. I shook my head in wonder and disgust.

"You know, Mom, I kind of get you wanting to lord it over Tammy. She can be a pain in the butt, for sure. But why did you try to ruin *my* cake, too? What have I ever done to you?"

Mom scowled. "I done told you, Valiant. *I didn't.* That stuff what was in the little bottle of yours? It wasn't nothing to ruin your cake. It was the last of Justas' moonshine. I wanted you to have it for your cake."

I wanted to speak, but that untamable wave of familial pride and shame crashed into my heart again. It clashed and thrashed in my mind like oil and water in a martini shaker, leaving me at a total loss for words.

"I...I –"

"Dale!" Mom hollered, interrupting my struggle.

Dale stumbled up to the table carrying a little jug.

"Dale, I told you not to get into that shed this morning!"

Dale was too tipsy to comprehend Mom's scolding. "Try a sip, Lucille."

"No!"

"Come on," Dale said, and thrust the jug at Mom. "I think you're gonna like this one."

"Let me see that," Mom said. She started to take a slug out of the jug, then stopped and looked me dead in the eye. "Mind you, Valiant, I never touch the stuff, being a good Southern Baptist. But this is for research."

Mom took a sip, swirled it around in her mouth and swallowed it. Her eyes wandered around as if she were searching the sky for something. She took another taste. This time her eyes lit up. "Well I'll be a golly washer, Dale. I think you've gone and done it!"

"Yeah? You for sure?" Dale asked, wide-eyed. "You ain't teasin' me now, Lucille. Is you?"

Mom handed him the jug. "Nope. That's it. That's it *perzactly.*"

"What are y'all talking about?" I asked as Dale took another slug.

"Looks like Dale done finally done matched up Justas' moonshine," Mom said.

Dale beamed with pride, but his feat didn't win him favor with Mom for long.

"All right, then. Now, Dale, when we gonna eat?" Mom demanded.

"Soon as me and Jake get the turkey heated up."

"Well then, what are you waiting for? Hop to it!"

TOM CAME BACK TO THE table after making his call. "Did I miss anything?" he asked.

"Just them two," Mom said, and pointed at her sisters.

Aunt Pansy and Aunt May sat down the table from us, four empty seats to the left. From the looks of them, they were still chewing their cuds about what went wrong with their fruitcakes, and how it was that Mom had managed to best them yet again. I wondered how long it would take for them to figure out they'd been done in by Elsie the magic cow, whose plastic udders gave glue instead of milk.

Mom raised her voice loud enough to ensure Aunt Pansy and Aunt May could hear. "In my family, Tom, we don't hide crazy folk. We give 'em a glass a tea and put 'em on the porch."

If looks could have killed, Mom would have been vaporized by Aunt Pansy and Aunt May right then and there. "Yeah? Well, at least I ain't no fart!" Aunt Pansy sneered.

"Fart?" Tom asked, then winced in anticipation of the explanation. Mom pursed her lips and left the explaining to me.

"Mom used to be a member of the Florida Association of Record Technicians. F-A-R-T."

Tom smirked, saw Mom's face and blanked his face to dead sober.

"I hope good Ol' Saint Nick brings you a dose of good ol' arsenick," Aunt May yelled.

Mom's face took on the smugness of a petty dictator. "Don't mind her, Tom," she said. "She's just jealous. Her son Freddie ain't got enough cents to pay attention, you know."

"Well, I never!" Aunt May screeched. She stood up and stomped off. Mom grinned like a redneck Cheshire cat.

I rolled my eyes and turned to Tom. "What did the guys have to say?"

Tom smiled politely at my mother, then said to me, "I'll tell you later."

"Why don't you two go do something useful," Mom groused. "Go see how Dale's doing with that dad-burn turkey. I'm hungry!"

Tom grabbed my hand and pulled me from the table. After we'd cleared a few feet, he whispered, "Geeze! Your family sure knows how to hold a grudge. At least now I know you come by it honest."

I jerked my hand from Tom's. "Are you saying I'm like them?"

"What? No. I mean, you're a drop in the bucket compared to them, Val."

I opened my mouth before my brain had a chance to process the information. Luckily, the comeback forming in my mind was waylaid by Uncle Jake on the megaphone.

"We have an announcement! Honorable Judge Tabitha Barfield has made a decision!"

The crowd grew quiet. Everyone turned and stared as Tabitha took the megaphone. "Thank you ladies and gentlemen," she said, careful to avoid eye contact. She looked down and read from her notebook. "After tallying up all the various points...

A commotion to my left caught my eye. Dale, legally blind and now tipsy as a toad, stumbled across the yard between the buffet table and the shed. He headed right for Uncle Jake's deep fryer. In his arms he toted a huge turkey. The plastic packaging was still on it, and it was covered in frost. Dale dropped the frozen bird into the boiling oil.

...the winner of this year's Family Fruitcake Frenzy is –"

KABOOM!

The deep fryer exploded, jettisoning the frozen turkey with a deep, hollow, "thwumping" sound akin to a huge firework going off. Like an organic IBM missile, the flaming turkey shot right through the open door of the shed. A second later, another explosion shook the ground, and tiny pieces of Mary Ann and the shed's tin roof rained down on us like yard sale manna from heaven.

Chapter Thirty-Three

"WHAT HAPPENED?" DALE wheezed as we picked him up off the lawn.

"Apparently, frozen turkeys and deep fryers don't mix," Tom said.

I brushed Dale off. Besides a few twigs in his hair and shortness of breath, he was unharmed. By some miracle, his flannel shirt, thick glasses, baseball cap and oven mitts had provided him with adequate protection.

"Lord! Dale!" Mom cried as she ran up to us, her face wracked with fear. "He ain't dead is he?"

"He's all right," I said. "Just got the wind knocked out of him."

Mom patted Dale's face. "You old fool," she said. Then she looked up at Tom and me and her demeanor changed back to normal, as if she'd flipped a switch in her heart. "He could'a killed us all! What happened?"

"I knowed it felt awful cold," Dale said, trying to recall the moments before the blast. "Jake was havin' to do all that announcing stuff with the megaphone. So he left me in charge of reheating that fried turkey of his. He told me he'd set it in the deep freezer in the shed so's no varmints could get to it. I guess when I went to fetch it out, I picked up the wrong one."

Dale hiccoughed, making Mom scowl.

"That moonshine you drunk didn't help, neither," Mom scolded. "I guess we can kiss *that* goodbye, too."

Tom picked up a pink funnel from the ground. I wagged my eyebrows at him. "Bye-bye, Mary Ann."

Mom stuck her finger in her ear and twisted it. "Did anybody hear whose fruitcake won? I think that dang explosion done took out my hearing aide."

I glanced around the crowd, but all I saw was a sea of dazed faces, and Aunt Pansy busily picking shrapnel out of her fruit salad.

AFTER ASSESSING THE minor damages to kinfolk, side dishes and fruitcakes, everybody decided it was time to get on with the Jolly family Christmas lunch, such as it was. We all worked our way along the buffet spread, setting any explosion debris in little piles between the dishes. At the end of the table, carved into heaps of dark and light meat, was Uncle Jake's fried turkey. It was cold, but the deep freezer had shielded it from the explosion.

"Let the Christmas Buffet commence!" Uncle Jake announced over the megaphone as we all took our places around the folding tables.

Hoots and hollers sounded around the table. We all raised our glasses of sweet tea to make a toast.

"To family!" Uncle Jake said. "Can't live with 'em, can't live without 'em."

"To family!" everyone hollered.

"And now, without further ado, Miss Tabitha Barfield will finish announcing the winner of this year's Family Fruitcake Frenzy."

Tabitha started to stand up, but fell back in her seat again. No doubt she was tipsy from all that boozy cake tasting.

"I see Tabitha's off her meds again," Mom sneered.

Tabitha's second attempt at standing was more successful. She wobbled as she took the megaphone. "Thanks again to all who participated," she began. "This year's winning fruitcake belongs to...Lucille Jolly-Short...

The crowd groaned. Mom grinned like Freddie Kruger.

...*and* Miss Val Fremden. *It's a tie!*"

I heard someone scream, but I couldn't tell who it was amongst all the cheers and hoots and hollers.

"Yeeesssss!" I shouted. I shot Mom a smirk and a waggled my head at her.

"Careful, there Val," Mom groused. "That high horse you're ridin' makes your butt look bigger."

I laughed out loud. Not even Mom was going to take this victory away from me. I grinned and kissed Mom on the cheek. "Looks like you're gonna have to learn to share, Mom."

Mom turned her nose up and wiped my kiss away.

"It wasn't an easy call," said Tabitha as she walked up to us. "Lucille, you got taken down a notch by that pecan shell. You might be slipping."

Mom grunted.

"And Val, your fruitcake was a hum-dinger. It went down like a fat kid on a greasy slide. But it didn't quite have that...that 'certain something.'"

Mom smirked to herself, then her face went sad. That "certain something" had just been blown to smithereens.

AS WE CLEANED UP THE aftermath of yet another festive holiday bloodletting, Tom was brimming with unanswered questions. As we washed up some of the surviving dishes, Tom and I had a chance to catch up and relive the highlights of the day.

"What was all that with the Tammy meltdown?" Tom asked. "The shopping bags of booze?"

"The way I see it, Tammy bought out the spiced rum at my Publix in hopes I couldn't find any more, thus ruining my chances of re-making my fruitcake. Either that or she was going to use it herself. But then she found out about the castor oil."

"Right," Tom said. "The castor oil. What was up with that?"

"Same strategy, different grocery store. Mom tricked Tammy into thinking castor oil was her secret winning ingredient."

Tom grimaced. "Castor oil?"

"Hey, like Mom said. You can't fix stupid. Speaking of stupid, your phone call with the guys. The mayor's place. What's up with that?"

"Goober told me about Rich's 'big job' at the mayor's." Tom shook his head. "You won't believe it. The guy's in charge of taking care of the mayor's dog, Val. Rich is a human pooper scooper."

"Yuck! But wait. How did Goober know that about Rich?"

"Goober said Rich handed him a flyer about a lost dog."

"Still, how did Goober know who Rich was?"

"He didn't. But when Goober described the guy's nose...." Tom made a face that finished his sentence.

"Gee. That's too bad. I was kind of hoping Rich would be the guy for Tammy."

Tom smiled and kissed me. "That's pretty charitable of you. And, hey. You never know. He still may be."

A thought hit me like a hammer between the eyes. I pulled away from Tom. "I didn't get you anything!"

Tom jumped back, startled. "What?"

"For Christmas. I didn't get you anything. I...I just wanted to come clean now. I thought about a pocket knife. Then it seemed so lame...."

Tom laughed and hugged me tight. "Val, you don't need to get me anything. This trip has been enough."

I cringed and looked into his sea-green eyes. "Well, you *did* survive. That's a gift, in a way, right?"

"It has certainly been memorable, I'll give you that. And, as I recall, you *did* promise me it was going to be a blast."

I WENT TO BED THAT night relieved. I'd survived another Christmas at my mother's. I was all settled in, snug on the couch when I heard my cellphone buzz. It was Milly.

"Merry Christmas, Milly."

"Merry Christmas, Val! I'm engaged!"

"What? Engaged?"

"Yes!"

"I'm so...so *happy* for you."

"You sound more worried than happy."

"I'm sorry. It's just so *surprising*. And *soon*. I don't want you to get in over your head, Milly."

"I'm tired of using my head, Val. Love isn't logical. And it doesn't run on some imaginary schedule. It just happens, even when you don't want it to."

"Okay. But answer me this, Milly. How do you know Vance is the one?"

"I don't know. It's like...have you ever talked on the phone with somebody you've never met, then one day you meet that person and they don't look anything like you imagined?"

"Uh...yeah, I guess."

"Val, love is like that. Somehow your heart *knows* who that one special person is. You might not know them when you *see* them, but you know them when you *feel* them. Does that make sense?"

"Kind of, but not really."

"Exactly!"

I laughed. "It sounds like you've found the perfect guy, Milly. I'm happy for you and Vance. Tell him Merry Christmas from me."

"I will. Merry Christmas, Val."

I clicked the phone off, set it on the coffee table and lay back on the couch. I truly *was* happy for Milly. Unlike me, she knew what she wanted. I settled into the covers. After all the anxiety I'd caused myself with my crazy thoughts about marriage, Tom hadn't bought me a ring after all. Part of me was disappointed, but a big part of me was relieved.

I closed my eyes and sighed. I was in the clear for another year. All of a sudden, joy shot through me like an electric charge. My eyes flew open and an ear-to-ear grin spread across my face. *I'd kicked Mom's butt in the fruitcake competition! Woo hoo!*

Chapter Thirty-Four

"I WANT YOU TO KNOW that I had me a big time," Tom said as he hugged Mom and Dale goodbye.

I smiled at Tom's effort to speak redneck as we stood at the front door, suitcases packed, itching to get on with our trip back home. I patted Dawson on the head. The old hound looked a lot perkier this morning. He'd survived his fruitcake hangover. Mom, however, was another story. I could tell she was stewing about our tie in the Family Fruitcake Frenzy. The news had swept through the family grapevine like wildfire, and the calls she'd received yesterday had been somewhat less than congratulatory.

I hugged Mom. She stiffened in my arms. "Thanks for everything," I said.

"Harrumph," she grunted.

Tom eyed me, grinned, and shook Dale's hand. "What's the secret to a happy marriage, Mr. Short?"

Dale squinted up at Tom through his thick lenses. "Moonshine, son. It'll make you do things you regret...but then it'll make you forget 'em, too."

"Regrets!" Mom snorted. "Regrets ain't any more use than standing on your tippy-toes to reach your own zipper."

"Oh!" Dale exclaimed and looked my way. "I almost forgot to give you your Christmas present, Val." He padded off in the direction of the kitchen.

"Here's yours from me," Mom said, and grudgingly handed over the petrified fruitcake trophy.

"Thanks, Mom. But...I didn't get you anything."

"You came. Like you said you would," Mom said flatly. "That'll have to do."

I pushed the fruitcake back into her hands. "Here. You keep it, for now."

Mom's sour face sweetened a notch. As she shoved the fruitcake under her arm, Dale ambled back, toting two moonshine jugs. "I squeezed two jugs outta Mary Ann before the blast," he said.

"What?" I asked. "Is this...the new *Justas juice?*"

Dale nodded with pride. "Yep. And it's all yours, Val."

"Thank you, Dale!" I hugged his slender frame, then took a jug and handed it to Tom. As I reached for the other jug, Mom swatted my hand away.

"Nothin' doin'," Mom barked. "Dale Short, one of them's *mine*."

She grabbed the second jug out of his hand and stared me down. Her cross, pouting face was no surprise, but her eyes caught me off guard. They hinted at...oh my word...*respect!* My mouth fell open.

"Now we're even, Val," Mom grunted. She nodded once and grinned at me like an unhinged bounty hunter. "May the best fruitcake win...*next year*."

TOM AND I PILED OUR luggage into his SUV and climbed inside the escape pod. He put his hands on the steering wheel and looked over me. "Are you okay?"

"I guess. Why?"

"'Cause you look kind of stunned. Or sad. Wait a minute. Are you *sorry* to leave?" He winked at me. "They warned me that redneck roots can run deep."

I sneered. "Not that deep."

Tom laughed. "Even though it comes off looking like a grudge match, Val, your family loves you, you know."

I smiled sourly. "Start the car, Tom. Let's get out of here before the humidity puffs up my hair like Jiffy Pop."

Tom shot me a grin. "You know, that Ricky was right."

"What do you mean?"

Tom laid on his best redneck accent. "He told me you was a keeper."

I laughed and backhanded his thigh. "Shut up!"

"All right. Just sayin'." Tom kissed me, shifted into drive and pulled onto the dirt road.

As we bumped along the ruts in the red clay, I realized Tom was right. I *was* sad to leave. But I was also grateful as hell to be getting out of Hicksville. I breathed a long sigh of relief, as if I'd awoken from a nightmare and remembered I actually *had* passed all my final exams.

I relaxed and settled myself in for the long drive home. But the peaceful, easy feeling didn't last long. We'd barely made it to the paved road when Tom punch me in the gut with a question from out of the blue.

"Val, do you know anything about the guys making a pet crematorium in their backyard?"

I jerked up in my seat. "Uh...what?"

Tom eyed me in his cop kind of way. "When I talked to Goober yesterday. He said Winky almost ate a cat leg off the grill. Jorge stopped him just in time. What the heck's going on there?"

At that instant my cellphone rang, like a post-Christmas miracle.

"Wait a minute," I said, and clicked the green answer button. "It's Winky. You can ask him about it yourself. I'll put him on speaker."

"Hey, there, you two! Merry Christmas!" Winky's voice blared out from my phone. Tom and I smiled at each other.

"Merry Christmas, Winky," I answered back. "Did you and the gang have a good one?"

"We sure did. Not to brag nor nothin', but we become kind a famous whilst you two was up there gallivanting around."

"What do you mean?" I asked.

"Well, you remember that story about us Three X-migos in the *Beachcomber Busy Bee* paper?"

Tom shot me a "What-the-hell?" stare.

"Yes...," I said.

"Well, that there story got us enough work lined up to keep us busy 'til New Year's."

"That's great."

"That ain't all. Yore gonna love this, Val. When me and Winnie got back from Lakeland, we wasn't ten minutes in the door when the dad-burned doorbell rang. It was that reporter gal, from the *Bee*, back to do what she called a 'follow-up.' Well, I thanked her kindly for her article, and told her that due to the publicity of it and all, me and the fellers prob'ly didn't have to do no more pet cremations to make ends meet."

I exchanged horrified looks with Tom. "Winky! You didn't!"

"I shore did! You two should'a been there! That lady's eyes lit up like a drunk on a beer-mas tree! She started asking all kind a questions about what we was up to. I give her the grand tour. Even showed her the grill."

I cringed. "But not the freezer, right?"

Tom shot me a "Who *are* you?" look.

"Gaul-dang it, Val, that was the best part!" Winky bellowed. "I nearly fell out laughing when I opened the freezer door. That woman screamed louder'n you did. Then she fainted dead away. But I got to hand it to her. She was a true professional, I tell you. When she come to, she got over it real quick-like, and wrote down all the details."

"Winky...that might not have been such a good idea...."

"Why not, Val? I figured there what'n no harm, seeing as how Hap-Pet-Ly Ever After was run by a bona fide officer of the law. It ought to have been on the up-an-up and all that."

"A police officer?" Tom asked, his voice cracking. "Who?"

"Well, Hans Jergen, a-course," Winky answered. "Didn't Val show you the picture of old Hans at the party?"

"What?" Tom yelped. He looked me in the eye. "You *knew* Hans Jergen was behind that?"

Winky answered before I could stutter out a reply. "Yep. And when that reporter lady found out old Hansy was the son of the police chief, she took to hootin' and hollerin' like a regular ol' hillbilly!"

"Oh dear lord," Tom moaned.

"But I guess it wasn't so legit as we thought, Val. Come to find out, this morning they fired old Hans Jergen for 'conduct unbefitting an officer.' I seen it on the news. Poor feller looked like a pit bull on death row."

"Geeze," Tom muttered and shook his head.

"Well, like they say, if the suit fits, wear it," Winky said. "But don't feel too bad about it Tom. They said on TV that after Jergen pays a $10,000 bond, he'll be released on his own repugnance."

My face cracked a tiny smile. I couldn't help but snicker. "How appropriate."

"Listen," Winky said. "I gots to go. Let's get together when you two get back in town."

"Sure thing." I clicked off the phone. Tom pulled his SUV to the side of the road, his knuckles white on the steering wheel.

"You *knew?*" Tom he growled.

"I only found out on the way up here," I whined in my defense. "I figured it could all wait until after Christmas. I was going to check it out before I bothered you with it."

"Before you *bothered* me?" Tom shook his head. "That's not the reason. You wanted to play Valiant Stranger. You wanted to investigate this on your own, didn't you?"

"You make it sound like...it wasn't like that –" I pleaded.

Tom stared, his face blank and resolved. "After all the trouble these exploits get you into, you can't give them up. Admit it."

"Well...okay. Maybe there's a tiny bit of truth to that, Tom. But I wanted to make sure of the facts. I mean, who would believe that a police lieutenant would moonlight as a cat cremator?"

Tom studied me with an unreadable glare. I bit my lip and thought about spilling my guts. Should I tell him about how I'd read through Jergen's tax returns earlier in the year and found out about Pet Patrol? How Pet Patrol turned out to be the business behind Hap-Pet-Ly Ever After? How I knew something bad was up because the mere mention of Pet Patrol to Jergen had been threatening enough to get him off Tom's back? But from the look on Tom's face, I could have been pouring gasoline on the fire....

"I'm sorry, Tom. I meant well. Honest. I mean, what *should* I have done?"

"I don't know," Tom barked. He shook his head at me, bewildered. "Cat cremator," he whispered. "Lord almighty." Then, like a dam breaking loose, the tension in Tom's face let go. He snickered once, then burst out laughing. Relieved, I laughed along with him. And when our eyes met, we lost it. We screamed with laughter, and kept on laughing and laughing until our bodies shook and we could laugh no more.

JUST OUTSIDE GREENVILLE, we stopped on Highway 90 to get gas. While Tom topped off the tank, I took the opportunity to scout out some local delicacies.

"Want and RC Cola and a moon pie?" I asked as I climbed out the passenger side door.

"Sounds great," Tom said. "Grab me a banana one, if they've got it."

I grinned. "I'm sure they will."

The shabby little convenience store didn't disappoint. As I climbed back into the SUV beside Tom with the colas and moon pies, Tom ambushed me. He thrust a small, unwrapped box toward me just as I took a sip of RC. I saw it and spewed cola all over the dashboard like a burst pipe.

Tom shook his head. "Val Fremden, you are the craziest, most messed-up woman I have ever met."

"Thanks," I mumbled as I wiped my face with a paper napkin. I looked him in the eye and shook my head. "Like I said before, Tom. I didn't get you anything." I eyed the box in his hand warily as I blotted the dashboard with the napkin.

"I love you, Val. Will you marry me?"

"What?" I almost got whiplash looking up at Tom. I glanced at the box, then back at Tom. Panic seized hold of my brain. "Do you...will you...I mean, are you just asking because my mom forced you to?"

Tom pulled back the box and looked at me sideways. "So you *did* hear that conversation."

Guilt forced my eyes downward. "Yes."

"Then you know."

I looked up. "Yes, my sister's illegitimate."

Tom laughed, "No, you nut! You know that my intentions are honorable." Tom opened the box. Inside was a gorgeous, blue, baguette-cut sapphire ring.

"That doesn't look like a normal engagement ring," I said.

Tom smirked and shook his head. "You're not a normal woman, Val."

I frowned.

"I meant that in the best possible way," Tom added.

I tried to smile, but I felt nauseous. "Does our relationship have to mean *marriage*, Tom? I mean...couldn't we keep our own places? Stay single, but *together?*"

Tom looked taken aback. "You don't want to?"

"I've seen a lot of happily-ever-after's end with marriage."

"You mean *in* marriage?"

"No. *With* marriage."

Tom twisted his lips sideways. "Well, I can't argue with that. But I'm an old-fashioned guy, Val Fremden. Think about it."

Tom slipped the ring on my finger and kissed me. I stared at the glimmering blue stone as Tom started the engine. We rode together in silence for a few minutes, until the SUV got to a stop sign at the junction of Highway 90 and US 221. Tom slammed on the brakes, startling me.

"Look," he said, and pointed out the windshield.

A green directional sign glared back at us. Silent and impartial, it stood like a beacon, offering Tom and me two paths from which to choose. Left would head us toward Donaldsonville, the home of Aunt May's drive-through chapel of matrimony. Right would lead us back to St. Petersburg, the place that had healed my heart. In other words, the place where anything was possible.

Tom smirked and raised his eyebrow a notch. "So, what do you say, Val? Which way from here? Left or right?"

I toyed with the ring on my finger. "I've never been to Donaldsonville..."

Tom grinned and opened his mouth to speak, but I cut him off.

"...but last time I checked, I still had a few spots left on my punch-card in Florida."

Tom nodded softly and shot me that boyish grin I'd come to love so much. "The choice is up to you, Val."

I leaned forward and kissed Tom. He was right. The choice was completely up to me.

DEAR READER,

Thanks so much for going home for the holidays with me in *What Four*! I hope you enjoyed the story. Bet you're feeling a little better about your own family right about now...lol!

My mission in What Four was to take a wacky, sideways view of the people who are close at heart – so close they can break our hearts without trying. I'm talking, of course, about family. But who qualifies as family, anyway? The people who gave you some genes, or the people who think you look good in your jeans? In Val's case, finding out she's not genetically related to her family was the biggest holiday gift of them all. Can you relate? I'm pleading the fifth on this one....

If you'd like to know when my future novels come out, please subscribe to my newsletter. I won't sell your name or send too many notices to your inbox.

Newletter Link: https://dl.bookfunnel.com/fuw7rbfx21

Thanks again for reading my book! What Four? For the laughs, of course! ;)

Sincerely,

Margaret Lashley

P.S. If you'd like to check out the next book in the series, Five Oh, I've included a sample for you in the back of this book. Or click here:

https://www.amazon.com/dp/B078BHWQPR

P.S.S. I live for reviews! The link to leave yours is right here:

https://www.amazon.com/dp/B075FS6ZKZ#customerReviews

P.S.S.S. (Sounds like I sprung a leak!) If you'd like to contact me, you can reach me by:

Website: https://www.margaretlashley.com

Email: contact@margaretlashley.com

Facebook: https://www.facebook.com/valandpalspage/

What's Next for Val?

*I hope you enjoyed What Four: Family Fruitcake Frenzy. Click
the link below now and leave a review. I read every single one!*

https://www.amazon.com/dp/B075FS6ZKZ#customerReviews
Thank you so much! You rock!

DON'T MISS ANOTHER new release! Follow me on Amazon and
BookBub and you'll be notified of every new crazy Val adventure.

Follow me on Amazon:

https://www.amazon.com/-/e/B06XKJ3YD8

Follow me on BookBub:

https://www.bookbub.com/search/authors?search=Mar-
garet%20Lashley

Ready for more Val?

*She survived the holidays – just barely! But Tom's still pressing hard
for a wedding. Is it time to get the shotgun?*

Enjoy the following excerpt from the next Val Fremden Mystery:

Five Oh: Fifty is the New F-Word!

Five Oh Excerpt

Chapter One

I THOUGHT I SAW A DWARF sneaking out of Laverne's house last night. But I could have been wrong. It was dark. And I was hopped up on Nyquil.

Funny. Yesterday, I'd started the day feeling *lucky*. I'd survived my mother's "holiday hospitality" with most of my self-worth intact – and my boyfriend Tom and I'd made the journey home without a hitch.

Well, that wasn't quite true. There had been *two* hitches. But compared to the family fruitcake disaster I'd just lived through, they'd weighed in as pretty minor. After all, they were just a close brush with death and a marriage proposal.

YESTERDAY, DURING THE ride home from Greenville, redneck capital of...*the world*, a rotten virus had snuck up and walloped me in the head like a Rock'Em Sock'Em Robot. It was the second sucker-punch to knock me for a loop that day. The first had been when my boyfriend Tom surprised me with an engagement ring. After spewing a mouthful of RC Cola all over the dash of his truck like a sprinkler-head gone haywire, my mind had seized up with an all-too-familiar uncertainty. For the life of me, when it came to the idea of matrimony, I couldn't decide whether to laugh for joy or scream with terror.

I knew marrying Tom was *my* choice, but I wasn't ready to make it. Not yet. All I'd known for certain at that moment was that I hadn't wanted to disappoint Tom. So I'd smiled, swallowed my fears, and played along with the engagement – then tried my best not to crap my pants before we got back home to St. Pete Beach.

During the five-hour drive, I'd felt increasingly weak and wobbly. By the time we reached Lake City, the anxiety that clouded my mind had grown so thick and heavy I could barely hold my head up. Somewhere around Ocala, my throat began to burn like fire. Hot pressure built up in my nose. Beads of sweat burst out above my lip.

That's when I knew for sure I hadn't been swept off my feet by love. I'd been done in by the flu.

I'd never been a good patient. Yesterday had proved that point again in spades. A tsunami of grouchiness had overtaken me. By the time poor Tom finally got me home, I'd been crabby enough to destroy Tokyo. He'd dropped me and my suitcase at the front door and fled. A veritable drive-by, dump-off. Who could blame him?

In all fairness to Tom, I'd begged him to leave me to wallow in my own wretchedness last night. There was no point in him getting sick, too. And I sure as heck didn't need him around to witness my hideous transformation into the red-eyed monster from planet Phlegm.

So, I'd stumbled into my house alone last night and collapsed onto my bed. I was beyond miserable. And, of course, I couldn't sleep. Around 2 a.m., I'd been in the bathroom slugging back my fourth shot of Nyquil when I'd heard a strange sound. With nothing else pressing on my agenda at that moment, I'd squandered what was left of my energy and dragged myself into the living room and peeked between the slats in the blinds.

That's when I thought I saw the dwarf sneaking down Laverne's driveway. But like I said, it was dark. And it could have been the Nyquil. The last time I'd taken the stuff I'd mistaken the mailman for Elvis.

A LIGHT TAPPING AT my front door woke me from a shallow, fitful sleep. I cracked open a crusty eye. My retina was instantly seared by the laser-white light radiating around the edges of the bedroom blinds like a million-megawatt picture frame. I squeezed my eye shut and groaned.

"*Ughh...*"

The tapping came again. Louder and more persistent this time. Absolutely no part of my body whatsoever wanted to move. But, as usual, I was overridden by ingrained Southern guilt. *I couldn't not answer the door, for heaven's sake!*

"Dang it!" I threw back the covers and drug myself out of bed. I wrapped my freezing body in my ratty bathrobe and fumbled down the hallway. One blurry, bloodshot eye strained to focus through the front-door peephole. A tall, thin, old lady with strawberry blond curls and a donkey face came into view. She stood at the door grinning like a chimp with a banana-split hangover. It was my next-door neighbor, Laverne Cowens. I sighed and opened the door.

"Hey, Laverne," I rasped. "Just so you know, I could be highly contagious."

"Highly who? I thought you were my neighbor, Val Fremden," Laverne joked.

"Huh," I grunted. Through my stuffy nose, it sounded more like "honk."

The twinkle in her bulgy eyes faded a notch as she studied my face. A sympathetic pout formed on her lips. "Awe, honey. I was just trying to be funny. You look awful!"

"Thanks." I blew what was left of my brains into a sodden tissue.

"You crawl back into bed. I'll make you some chicken soup."

"You don't have to –"

"Nonsense!" Laverne clomped inside on her gold high heels. She shooed me toward my bedroom with a thin, liver-spotted hand. "Just tell me one thing first, honey. Where's your can opener?"

The right side of my mouth curled upward. I flailed a weak arm in the direction of the kitchen. "Third drawer to the left."

"All righty, then. Scoot!"

I shuffled my way down the hall toward the bathroom as Laverne banged my pots and pans around like a naughty two-year-old. I avoided my reflection in the vanity mirror. I felt sick enough already.

In my addle-brained state, I thought if I could brush my matted hair, I'd feel better. I picked up the brush and forced it into my hair. It stuck in place like it was covered in Crazy Glue. *Great.* I yanked the brush out of the rat's nest encircling my head and fumbled my way back to bed.

As I lay there pondering the idea that death might be a pleasant option, that crazy old lady who lives next door managed to make me laugh. From the kitchen, Laverne, bubble-headed sage and former Vegas showgirl, was belting out a horrendously off-key rendition of *Zippity Do Da*, punctuating it randomly with an occasional, "Gosh, dang it!"

I sighed and relaxed into the bed covers as my fevered mind envisioned Laverne doing the can-can with a can of soup in each hand.

I was lying on an operating table. A masked doctor held my detached heart up to the light.

"What's your opinion?" the doctor asked the man next to him, a clown wearing a brown derby hat with a daisy sticking out of it.

"Lederhosen," the clown said.

"Just as I suspected," the masked surgeon said. "Get her out of here."

An orderly appeared from the mist, looking suspiciously like Sasquatch in blue scrubs. He grabbed my foot and started yanking it....

I woke with a start. Laverne was standing at the foot of my bed, shaking my left foot through the bedspread.

"Hey, honey. Wake up. Soup's on." She held my big blue mixing bowl in her hands. "Eat up. Then I want to hear all about your trip to your mom's."

Laverne watched me patiently, grinning in her mother donkey sort of way, as I hauled my body to sitting and settled myself in amongst the bed pillows.

"Where do I start?" I groaned.

"Why, at the beginning, of course." She stretched her long, spidery arms across the bed to hand me the bowl of soup. As I reached for it, she stopped midway, leaving my fingers grasping feebly at the air like a toddler begging to be picked up.

"Where'd you get that?" she asked.

"Get what?"

"That ring."

"Oh." I winced weakly. "Tom gave it to me. I guess...we're...*engaged*, sort of."

Laverne eyed the ring dubiously. "It doesn't *look* like an engagement ring."

"I know. It's a blue sapphire. Tom said it was unusual, because *I'm* so unusual."

"Huh. Let me see it."

I held my hand out.

"No," Laverne said. "I mean take it off. Let me *see* it."

I did as I was told. Laverne set the bowl of soup on the nightstand, grabbed the ring and held it up to the ceiling light. One bulgy eye squinted as the other opened wide to study the inside the band. "It's engraved," she needlessly informed me. "I Luv U. *Aww.* L-U-V." She looked over and shot me a full-denture grin. "How sweet!"

"Yeah. Don't remind me," I said grumpily. "It's pretty sappy. And the dumb spelling doesn't help, either. But I've decided to chalk it up to lack of space, rather than Tom's lack of taste."

Laverne's smiling face wilted like a plucked daisy in the sun. "Tom's a good guy, you know."

I sighed. "I know. I'm sorry. I'm just not feeling the greatest right now."

"Sure. That's it," Laverne said, and perked back up. "Eat your soup. It'll help."

I leaned across the pillows and reached sideways for the soup. As I did, my elbow hit the bowl and knocked it halfway off the nightstand. Laverne and I gasped and watched in slow-motion horror as the soup teetered precariously on the edge of the table.

"I got it," I cried, and tried to grab the bowl from the bottom. But I overreacted and swatted the bowl upward instead. It did a back flip, bounced off the nightstand and hit the rug with a wet thud. A quart of chicken-noodle soup splattered all over the place.

"Oh, crap," I groaned, and sank back into the pillows.

"My lordy!" Laverne said. She crinkled her nose at the mess and handed me back my engagement ring. I groaned, slipped it on my finger, then tried to get out of bed.

"What are you doing?" Laverne demanded.

"Gotta...clean up...this mess," I mumbled.

"Nothin' doin! It wasn't your fault, honey. No use crying over spilled soup. I'll fetch you another bowl and then clean this up myself."

"But..."

"No buts! It's not so bad, sugar. And you need to rest." Laverne studied me for a moment, then winked. "And if you finish your soup, young lady, you can have a piece of cherry pie."

My heart lurched in my congested chest. Laverne's cooking skills were legendary – in the way Jack the Ripper was legendary for making house calls.

"Did *you* make the pie?" I asked.

"Sure did!" Laverne beamed. "In my new cooking class. *Southern Classic Desserts.*"

My life flashed before my eyes. *Think of something, quick!* "Uh...thanks, Laverne. It sounds delicious. Really. But I have to pass. I have a wedding dress to fit into, remember?"

Laverne crinkled her nose, then brightened like a three-watt bulb. "Oh, that's right! I didn't think about that, sugar." She grinned and pointed an index finger toward the ceiling. "One new soup, coming up!" She spun on her high heels and bounced out the bedroom door.

I melted back into the pillows. Relief washed over me like a warm, Gulf tide. I'd narrowly evaded Laverne's cooking, and, so far, Tom's insistence on getting married. The dress I had to fit into wasn't for *my* wedding. It was for my best friend Milly's. She and Vance would be tying the knot in four months. I blew my swollen clown nose and sighed.

Better you than me, girlfriend. Better you than me.

Keep on reading! Grab your copy now with the link below!
https://www.amazon.com/dp/B078BHWQPR

About the Author

LIKE THE CHARACTERS in my novels, I haven't lead a life of wealth or luxury. In fact, as it stands now, I'm set to inherit a half-eaten jar of Cheez Whiz...if my siblings don't beat me to it.

During my illustrious career, I've been a roller-skating waitress, an actuarial assistant, an advertising copy writer, a real estate agent, a house flipper, an organic farmer, and a traveling vagabond/truth seeker. But no matter where I've gone or what I've done, I've always felt like a weirdo.

I've learned a heck of a lot in my life. But getting to know myself has been my greatest journey. Today, I know I'm smart. I'm direct. I'm jaded. I'm hopeful. I'm funny. I'm fierce. I'm a pushover. And I have a laugh that makes strangers come up and want to join in the fun. In other words, I'm a jumble of opposing talents and flaws and emotions. And it's all good.

In some ways, I'm a lot like Val Fremden. My books featuring Val are not autobiographical, but what comes out of her mouth was first formed in my mind, and sometimes the parallels are undeniable. I drink TNTs. I had a car like Shabby Maggie. And I've started my life over four times, driving away with whatever earthly possessions fit in my car. And, perhaps most importantly, I've learned that friends come from unexpected places.

Made in the USA
Columbia, SC
18 June 2020

11330729R00133